What people

"I loved reading it. Once I started, I couldn't put it down. I love the cover.........it's so Saipan-ish and eye catchy. And makes you want to read about the crazy Jamaican on Saipan!" It's, DA BOMB!" – Kim Capers

"I LOVE THE COVER! It captures the fantasy of living in paradise, and made me want to pick it up and read it!"
— Stacey Spencer-Willoughby

"This is wonderful! I absolutely love the photos and looked forward to hearing about your daily adventures. This is going to be a hit! It truly portrays the essence of living your dream and experiencing your vision to the fullest."—Adrienne

"...the rat story is crazy!"—F.W.

Five good reasons to own Jamaican On Saipan

1. It's hard enough getting a seat on the subway, and it's crowded enough without having to incur the wrath and nasty looks of other passengers as you open up a laptop to read an ebook. Paperbacks are convenient.

2. Your granny in the hills in St. Mary wouldn't use a computer to read a book even if you paid her. Paperbacks are easier.

3. You can lend it to someone to read and not worry that they'll find that secret folder on your hard drive. Paperbacks are safer.

5. It's only $14.95 when you order at www.JamaicanOnSaipan.com. Paperbacks are cheap.

FOR IMMEDIATE RELEASE:

SAIPAN, MP--With its world class diving sites, corals beyond compare, natural beauty, warm weather and people to match, the paradise-inspired island of Saipan in the north Pacific might be just the ideal setting for a nomad's adventure, except that few people are familiar with this furthest east American commonwealth just 150 miles north of Guam. But *Notes from a Jamaican on Saipan*, a new book by Walt Goodridge, which chronicles the author's escape from the rat race in search of a private dream, may yet change that fact.

"I wanted to tell a different story," Goodridge explains, "from a perspective and through eyes you don't normally experience." And he does indeed. Born in Kingston, Jamaica, and raised for half his childhood in Jamaica, New York, Goodridge, a self-described "mobile, mac-enabled, mimimalist nomapdreneur who happens also to be vegan" reveals a personal vision of happiness he'd been searching for all his life. His story begins with his challenging, almost aborted "escape from America," his arrival and acclimation to Saipan's unique culture and lifestyle, adapting as a vegan in a meat-centric paradise, finding opportunities for making money, achieving fame, and even cross-cultural dating on a Pacific island.

A graduate of Columbia University, a civil engineer who walked away from his career to be an entrepreneur, former radio personality, author of 14 books, e-business guru, public speaker and career coach, Goodridge amassed an impressive resume in his "former" life in the states. Even so, he's not afraid to risk baring the ignominy of some of his experiences on the other side of the world--such as one episode of having no money or credit card and having to call friends back in the states in the middle of the night for Paypal® loans to purchase a ticket, or his "rats in the kitchen" situation, or finding out too late that he hadn't done sufficient research to know that he needed a visa for travel to certain countries.

With its wide coverage of life on Saipan, the book also doubles as a travel guide, touching on a wide range of topics of interest to potential visitors, retirees, tourists and fellow nomads who will find his "notes" not just entertaining, but also educational, and a great way to round out one's knowledge of this relatively unknown, but quite unique island paradise. By the time you finish reading, you'll know enough about Saipan's culture, lifestyle, economy, tourist spots and even some of the local celebrities to feel like you've been there, or at the very least, to decide if you want to go.

Goodridge's story is a personal, inspiring, at times embarrassing often amusing, but never dull account of the adventure that life often gives as reward to those with the courage to live their dreams. With a Jamaican's eye for cultural anomaly, a coach's desire to teach, and a poet's way with words, Walt chronicles his year-long experience in a collection of personal emails, blog posts and private journal entries. The result is a hard-to-put-down adventure peppered with insightful observations and analysis on everything from global warming, to finding economic opportunity, love and happiness in paradise!

Jamaican on Saipan!

Updated for 2010!

*The True Story Of One Man's
Escape From The Rat Race
To Live A Personal Nomadpreneur's Dream!
(a unique travel guide for the rest of us)*

Walt F.J. Goodridge

The Passion Profit Company
a division of a company called W
NEW YORK. SAIPAN.

Walt Goodridge is...
Jamaican on Saipan!
The True Story Of One Man's Escape From The Rat Race To Live A Personal Nomadpreneur's Dream!(a unique travel guide for the rest of us)
Copyright © 2009 Walt F.J. Goodridge

All rights reserved. This book may not be reproduced in whole or in part, or transmitted in any form, without written permission from the author and publisher, except by a reviewer who may quote brief passages in a review. Contact: info@passionprofit.com
Educational institutions, government agencies, libraries and corporations are entitled to quantity discounts. Contact: orders@passionprofit.com

Cover Photo: *Walt at Forbidden Island, Saipan* taken by Angelo Villagomez

Published and distributed by:
The Passion Profit Company
P.O. Box 618, Church Street Station
New York, NY 10008-0618, USA
email: orders@passionprofit.com | web: www.passionprofit.com

Retail Cost: $14.95
ISBN-13: 978-0-9745313-9-7; ISBN-10: 0-9745313-9-1
Printed in the United States of America

Library of Congress Cataloging-in-Publication Data
Goodridge, Walt F. J.
  Jamaican on Saipan : the true story of one man's escape from the rat race to live a personal nomadpreneur's dream! : (a unique travel guide for the rest of us) / Walt F.J. Goodridge.
    p. cm.
  Includes bibliographical references.
  ISBN-13: 978-0-9745313-9-7 (pbk. : alk. paper)
  1. Saipan--Description and travel. 2. Goodridge, Walt F. J.--Travel--Northern Mariana Islands--Saipan. 3. Jamaicans--Northern Mariana Islands--Saipan--Biography. 4. Jamaican Americans--Northern Mariana Islands--Saipan--Biography. 5. Nomads--Northern Mariana Islands--Saipan--Biography. 6. Businessmen--Northern Mariana Islands--Saipan--Biography. 7. Businessmen--New York (State)--New York--Biography. 8. Saipan--Social life and customs. I. Title.
  DU648.S35G66 2007
  919.67--dc22
                                    2007018031

Dedicated to
my mother, Thelma Rose Goodridge
my father, Nyembane Ndobe Goodridge
and my grandmother,
Isolene Rebecca Golding

****

Dedicated also to the friends I made in Part I of my life in Jamaica from Old Harbour Primary School, Pembroke Hall Primary School and Hughenden Housing Scheme. These are the names I've never forgotten though I've lost touch with most:

Andrew Walters • Wayne Walters • Lisa Walters • Baron Brissett Horace Hall • Ian Smith • Daighn Jones • Sharon Hamilton Desmond Anderson • Ferdinand White • Norman Hemming Perez Cross • Germaine Gail Scott • Dion Thompson • Richard Polack • Mr & Mrs. Sutherland • Richard Sutherland Philip Sutherland • Mrs. Downy • Gary Scott • Mrs. Scott • Mr.. & Ms Nash • Tanya Nash • Mr. & Mrs. Johnson • Gillian Johnson • Paul Johnson • Mr. & Mrs. Samuels • Peter Samuels • Paul Samuels Lorraine Samuels • Sophia Samuels • Camille Samuels • Mr. & Mrs. Barton • Marcia Barton • Herbert Barton • Wayne Barton • Mr. & Mrs. Britain • Karen Britain • Avril Britain • The McDonalds • The McGregors • The Beckets • Carl Steadman

anyone out there? (walt@jamaicanonsaipan.com)
or find me on Facebook

And special appreciation to Saipan resident, Ruth Tighe, for her editorial input and suggestions.

Jamaican On Saipan!
Table of Contents

Foreword: Jamaican-ize	9
Introduction: Jamaican-eyes	10
A World Without Borders	12
Note 1: How it all Began	13
Note 2: Freedom Song	15
Note 3: Escape from New York	17
Note 4: Escape from Las Vegas	21
Note 5: Escape from Las Vegas, Take Two	29
Note 6: Escape from Japan	31
Note 7: Welcome to Saipan!	33
Note 8: Where on Earth is Saipan?	34
Note 9: Saipan Facts and Figures	36
Note 10: Off to a Great Start	38
Note 11: First Impressions	40
Note 12: Sights and Sounds...	48
Note 13: Passion Prophet in Paradise	51
Note 14: Meeting the Governor	53
Note 15: Elements of Fame	54
Note 16: Alien Soul	56
Note 17: Let the Music Play	59
Note 18: The Most Important Day of My Life	64
Note 19: Vegan in Paradise	65
Note 20: The Saipan Tribune	67
Note 21: MLK Day Legislation Passed	69
Note 22: Sistah Constable	70
Note 23: Settling In	71
Note 24: New York Calling...	74
Note 25: Rats in the Kitchen	74
Note 26: Dating, Language and Culture	77
Note 27: Return to New York	79
Note 28: Jamaican in Canada	81
Note 29: Preserving Paradise	82
Note 30: The 10 Commandments of Paradise	82
Note 31: Paradise-preneurs	85
Note 32: My World	91
Note 33: Walt's Friday Inspirations Ends	92
Note 34: Escape from America, the Sequel	94
Note 35: A Nomad Ruminates on Home	98

Note 36: Saipan Food Co-op	100
Note 37: Guam	103
Note 38: A Week in the Life	106
Note 39: Okay, So it's more than a week	110
Note 40: A Few Things I Haven't Done	111
Note 41: Heard and Seen on Saipan	112
Note 42: My Best Friend's Wedding	113
Note 43: Holidays on Saipan	118
Note 44: BeautifyCNMI!	121
Note 45: We Love Saipan!	123
Note 46: The Master Plan	125
Note 47: How We REALLY Did It	129
Note 48: MLK Day in the CNMI	130
Note 49: Early-Retirement on Saipan	133
Note 50: Island Fever?	134
Note 51: Saipan Calling	137
Note 52: Someone from the Future	138

Part Two! (2009 Update)

Note 53: There's always something to do	140
Note 54: The Best of Saipan!	147
Note 55: My Senate Resolution	148
Note 56: Contract Workers Unite	149
Note 57: Another Jamaican!	149
Note 58: MLK Traditions Continue	150
Note 59: Food for a Week on Saipan	152
Note 60: Marianas Trench Monument	153
Note 61: And Then, There's Obama!	155
Note 62: Ode to the Garment Factory	156
Note 63: Some Scenes We May Not See Again	159
Note 64: Chicken Feathers and Garlic Skin	160
Note 65: Federalization and the Visa Waiver	161
Note 66: The Truth About Saipan	162
Note 67: And Finally... A Better Life?	166
Note 68: The Final, Final Word	167
About the Author	168
Further Reading and Resources	169
Saipan on DVD!	170
Saipan in Paperback	171
Books and Products by Walt Goodridge	172
Quiz	172
Order Form	173

Key

(*Notes from a) Jamaican on Saipan* is a story told through a collection of blog entries, personal emails, excerpts from my newspaper column, and personal analyses. Here is a key:

   = *email received by me*

   = *email sent by me*

   = *my newspaper column*

Foreword: Jamaican-ize

From the people who brought you the Maroons, Marcus Garvey, Rastafari, Democratic Socialism, Reggae, Bob Marley, Cool Herc, Delroy Lindo, Colin Powell, Madge Sinclair, Grace Jones, Harry Belafonte, Shari Belafonte, Sheryl Lee Ralph, Oliver Samuels, Louise Bennett, Lennox Lewis, Busta Rhymes, Grace Jones, Heavy D, Notorious BIG, Donovan Bailey, Naomi Campbell, Stacey McKenzie, Tyson Beckford, "The Reggae Boyz" (the national team which made Jamaica the first English-speaking Caribbean country to qualify for World Cup football), Usain Bolt, and, of course, the Jamaican bobsled team, comes word of another Jamaican trendsetter:

Walt F.J. Goodridge

Jamaicans are known for their hardworking, entrepreneurial, adventurous and rebellious spirits—a stereotype, to be sure, but a welcome and arguably true one. Not content to a limited geographical circumscription or influence for its native sons and daughters, this little island in the Caribbean has produced politicians, sports figures and musicians who've had global influence. Today, there's probably not a spot on the planet where Jamaicans' presence and influence have not been directly or indirectly felt.

Well, you can now add the island of Saipan to the list of Jamaican-ized corners of the world! On this little island in the Pacific ocean, 8730 miles from Kingston, Jamaica, Walt Goodridge, author of 12 books, public speaker, career coach, poet, and self-described vegan, minimalist, nomadpreneur, brings a mixture of his home island's perspective and his own maverick ways to tell a unique story that goes beyond the expected. And while his career credits and chosen lifestyle bespeak a departure from the ordinary, Walt will tell you himself that *Jamaican On Saipan* is simply about an Old Harbour country boy and Kingston resident venturing out to see the world...through Jamaican eyes.

Introduction: Jamaican Eyes

The story of my life: My name is Walt Goodridge. I was born in Jamaica. My family migrated to America. I went to high school and college in the US. I graduated with a civil engineering degree from Columbia University. I worked in the corporate world for seven years. I became an entrepreneur, and then walked away from my engineering career. I left the states. This is the story of the first year of my international nomadpreneur adventure.

I wrote *Jamaican on Saipan* for several reasons.

First, I'm a writer, and that's what we writers do. And although I write business books, this time I wanted to tell a story that's less about being a business and career coach, and just about my life as an ordinary man following his private dream.

Second, while preparing for my trip to Saipan, I searched bookstores and realized that not only were the travel accounts from this unique region limited, but many often contained cultural biases I didn't share.

Think about it. A person's predispositions, her personality, background, experiences and expectations, even his height and size are all going to impact how she treats others and how others treat him in return. So, as a friend of mine who traveled to India recently told me, wearing shorts there is considered odd enough. Wearing shorts to visit a temple is almost sacrilege. So if an unaware tourist dons his shorts and sandals for sightseeing in India, what sort of experience might he have? Is it going to be positive? How will the residents there treat him? If he's a travel writer, will he then write about his experience in glowing terms?

By the same token, as a Jamaican from a climate and lifestyle, world-view, perspective and even physical appearance more similar to that on a Pacific island, how are my experiences going to differ? How will people treat me?

The eyes and life experiences through which you view the world, as well as the form through which the world views you will determine your experience in any land. Had I not been introduced to Saipan, or experienced it through my friend Ken's eyes, and had I based my impressions exclusively on travel guide accounts, or what I found on the internet, I might never have chosen it as a place to begin my nomad dream.

In addition, many travel guides are typically written for the benefit of tourists. However, like me, many of my friends, when traveling, like to see how residents live and what life is like for everyday folk who live there. That's what I like about visiting new places: not the "touristy" things that most guides will suggest, but the day-to-day experiences of life. However, *Jamaican on Saipan* is not a definitive travel guide, by any means. It's just my own personal story of a year in my life—the sort of travel guide I like to read. The phrase *"a unique travel guide for the rest of us"* is a tongue-in-cheek acknowledgement of that fact.

So who are the rest of us, you ask? In any given day or discussion, I may refer to myself as Jamaican, minimalist, vegan or nomadpreneur. I am a Jamaican who grew up in America, so I've lived on the outside looking in for most of my life. I am a minimalist, so I can live without the luxuries and amenities to which others may be accustomed. I am vegan, so the beliefs that inform my dietary choices make me aware of and sensitive to certain cultural norms others may miss. I am an entrepreneur, with a penchant for freedom, so I see things and new lands in terms of potential business opportunities that support a wanderer's lifestyle. While each facet of that identity, individually, may appear to limit the number of those to whom I can relate, it actually broadens the perspectives from which I can view the world. It gives me opinions, and equips me to make observations, connections and associations that a mainstream, nine-to-five, materialistic, omnivore may naturally overlook!

So while you may not share my vegan views, minimalist lifestyle, Jamaican background, nor be of an entrepreneurial bent with nomadic proclivities, the existence of these alternative perspectives may, if nothing else, tell a story you may find eye-opening, one you'll rarely hear....and one I hope you'll share.

Enjoy these notes from a Jamaican on Saipan!—Walt

A World Without Borders

"To create a just, sustainable world, nothing is more important than being able to think and act across borders. Whether our passion is protecting the biosphere or preventing war, we will succeed only if we have the passion and courage to cross the national, ideological, ethnic, and religious borders of our time."--Mark Gerzon, author of *Leaders without Borders*.

Note 1: How it all Began

It was all just one of those seemingly spontaneous, but subconsciously orchestrated decisions, stemming from a set of seemingly random, but divinely engineered events that led to my seemingly fortuitous, but cosmically predictable arrival on the island of Saipan.

In December of 2005, my friend Ken, who lived in Las Vegas, Nevada at the time, happened to be in Brooklyn, New York visiting a friend. He invited me to a holiday party that was to take place on Saturday, December 16, 2005.

When that Saturday rolled around, I made the long, late night train ride from Harlem to Brooklyn. After the party ended, at about 3:00 a.m. or 4:00 a.m. that Sunday morning, I was all set to leave, when we discovered that Ken's car was blocked in by a neighbor's. Ken suggested we knock on the neighbor's door, and request that she let us out. However, rather than wake the neighbor up so early on a Sunday morning, I suggested we simply chat and wait it out, as the sleeping neighbor would likely be up in a few hours to go to church.

After touching on a few random topics, we happened to get into a discussion about Ken's recent trip to Japan to produce some music for some Japanese artists. While there, the artists took Ken to Saipan to work with another producer on that island.

He had such a wonderful time that he went back again several months later. He revealed the details of his "good time" to me that night in Brooklyn. Something about it piqued my interest, sparked my curiosity, and stirred my latent nomadic streak, which I had kept submerged for all these years.

The hustle and bustle of life in New York City. Escape is imminent.

     The prospect of living life in a whole new world came at a time when, jaded by the materialism and crowded yet often isolated living of metropolitan life, I was seeking to reinvent myself. Ken's pitch contained all the right words and phrases: warm weather, beautiful people (read: women), slower lifestyle, all while still on the U.S. Postal System—a seemingly trivial, yet important consideration for my mail order business. Yes, something clicked, and I made a decision that night that I was Saipan-bound.

     I bought my ticket, gave away my 2500-strong vinyl lp collection, donated my books to a combination of friends and street vendors, unloaded almost everything I own, and jetted.

     Two months after that fateful conversation, I executed my escape from America. The date was February 23, 2006.

     I always think about the fact that had I not gone to that party that night, and we not opted to wait out the wee morning hours engaged in conversation, that the topic of travel and Saipan may not ever have come up, and present Saipan as an option for this now quite happy nomadpreneur. Ahhh, yes. What mightn't have been.

     But, let me go back a bit and fill in some of the details.

Note 2: Freedom Song

      Yep, after Ken's pitch, I was all set to make a drastic change in my life. I started doing research, sending emails requesting information, making connections on couchsurfing.com, and booking fares and accommodations for the journey. As the day of my departure got closer, I sent the following email to a few friends, customers and clients:

February 9, 2006
hi all,
      As you may have surmised, and as was hinted at in several of my recent Friday Life Rhymes* (specifically #437 entitled "Freedom Song"), something's been brewing in "Walt World" for the past few months.
      Ever since leaving corporate America in the fall of 1995, I've been executing a plan to create the lifestyle of a modern, minimalist, nomadic, passionpreneur based on a passive-residual income stream! In other words, I want out of the rat race!
      Now that I've cut all the tethers and structured a turnkey, self-sustaining, internet-based business that doesn't require my physical presence in any one location......(drum roll, please)
      ...I've bought a one way ticket to the island of Saipan in the South Pacific! [note: Saipan is actually in the Western Pacific, but South sounds so much more exotic]
      So amid sea, sand and sun, I'll be living my dream in a clime that resonates with who I wish to be.
      Since this is simply the first step in a journey of a thousand smiles, I didn't want to make a big deal about it until I got there and surveyed the lay of the land. But, I wanted to tell a few friends and contacts who I felt deserve a little advanced notice...
      You can still reach me at walt@passionprofit.com, and I'll set up a Skype™ account and MSN Messenger for IMs for anyone who'd like to keep in touch, and share the experience!

Walt
p.s. I leave next Wed February 15 for Las Vegas, and then I'm on to Japan—my first stop on the way to Saipan! If you know of anyone there in Tokyo I can call who might be kind enough to show me around, please let me know. And in case you didn't receive Life Rhyme* #437, here it is again:

Freedom Song

One day you'll think about me:
Haven't seen him in a while
You'll make a note to find me
or a number you can dial

One day you'll ask about me:
Where on earth can he be found?
And learn at last I've set my sail
where sun and sea abound

One day you'll say about me:
Goes the nomad on his way
To live the life's adventure
that he said he would some day

One day you'll write about me:
There's the man who lived his dream
Cut loose the oars and left the boat
to swim a different stream

And then one day amid the noise
and hustle of the throng
You'll hear a tune first faintly
that's been playing all along

You'll know the singer instantly
you'll recognize my voice
A heart-felt freedom song
of life lived not by chance but choice...

[end of email]

    And so began my escape from America. What follows is the real-time, day-to-day, step-by-step account of how it all transpired written on my laptop everywhere from airport lounges, hotel rooms and airplanes to beaches, buses, boats to wherever I call "home."

*Walt's Friday Life Rhymes are a weekly inspirational email I sent to my 10,000 subscribers for 9 years. The archives are at www.liferhymes.com

Note 3: Escape From New York!

February 15, 2006

My escape from America has begun!

It's now 1:00 p.m. on Wednesday, February 15, 2006. I'm sitting on an ATA Airlines flight bound to Chicago's Midway Airport—the first stopover on my way to Las Vegas.

Tell you a quick story. With my flight scheduled to leave New York's LaGuardia Airport at 12:15 p.m., I decided I had more than enough time to tie up a few loose ends around the city before I headed out. So, first I hopped on a subway train from Harlem to the 34th Street Post Office to send out some books to customers and to ship a box ahead to my final destination on Saipan. (I was told that if I shipped anything to Saipan from the US, I needed to send it via Priority Mail, for it to arrive in a reasonable time.) Then I headed down to the West Village to pick up a copy of *Tales from the Time Loop* by David Icke. Figured I needed some good conspiratorial reading to punctuate my escape from "the system!"

Now, don't ask me what I was thinking, but I fully expected the Barnes & Noble bookstore on 8th Street and 6th Ave to be open at 9:00 a.m. Seemed like a fairly traditional opening hour for a New York business.

Well, I got there at 9:20 a.m. only to discover that it wouldn't be open until 10:00 a.m. Drat! So I walked around The Village in hopes of finding another B&N or other bookstore that would be open earlier. I found the B&N Astor place store, but it, too, would open at 10:00 a.m. So then I walked over to Broadway, and up to 13th Street to Strand Bookstore, but they didn't carry any of Icke's books. So then I walked up to the 14th Street Virgin Megastore, but struck out there as well. Finally I ended up back at the 8th Street B&N. By that time it was 9:50 a.m. So I waited outside for the ten minutes until the security guard opened up at the stroke of 10.00am. I rushed upstairs, grabbed the book from the shelf of the New Age section, and bounded back downstairs to pay for it. It was now 10:05 a.m. With book in hand, I headed back up to Harlem to finish packing for my trip. I don't ever pack until the day of my flight; OK, so perhaps my priorities are a bit skewed.

Well, I got back home at 10:30 a.m. After throwing a few last-minute items into my bags, I left my apartment at 10:40 a.m. This was a snowy day in February. I trudged through the snow the six blocks to 125th street with my two suitcases and a backpack with my laptop. However, I wasn't done with my errands just yet. I still had to get some Aloe Ferox bitters from Watkins Health Food store on 125th St. So, leaving my bags out on the sidewalk under the watchful eyes of two complete strangers, I rushed in, made my purchase, and came out in time to catch the M60 bus to LaGuardia Airport. It was now 11:06 a.m. (Yes, I know my flight is at noon!)

When we pulled into LaGuardia's Central terminal, I disembarked, walked up to the counter, which was emptier than I expected. (Hmmm. wonder why?) And I sauntered casually up to the ticket counter attendant. She asked what flight I was on. I told her the 12:15 p.m. to Chicago, and she said, "Sorry, you missed it." (an obvious power play on her part. She obviously didn't realize who I was). So, I used a Jedi mind trick to have her call the baggage handlers to okay the arrival of my bags (which of course they did). She then scolded me for getting there late.

"Next time, you can't come this late, okay?" she said. (pause) "I'm serious!" she added for emphasis.

I wanted to tell her, "Lady, if things go as planned, there WON'T be a next time!" But I figured this wasn't the appropriate time or place to get into that discussion. She then printed my boarding pass, and tagged my bags. Actually, I tagged my bags after she *ordered* me to help her. She then instructed me to run like I was in a race to Gate B-4 if I wanted to catch my flight, since I still had the security checkpoint to go through. (I wanted to invoke the O.J. Hertz airport visual to her, but again, thought better of it). I got to security, where I cut the line thanks to a helpful gate attendant, got my bags x-rayed (I kept having thoughts of them confiscating my property to sell on eBay), and made it to the gate just as passengers were boarding, showed my boarding pass, and made my way to seat 28D, the very last seat right before the rest room, and coincidentally, right behind a family with a gang of babies who seemed all at once to be teething, purging, and trampolining.

So here I sit, typing this note, listening to "Could You Be Loved" by Bob Marley through my headphones, while being buffeted by the aroma of restroom excrement from behind, and baby diaper poo from up ahead. Ahhhh, but who's complaining? No one ever said escape would be easy!

Next stop: Chicago! Hmmm. Isn't that Oprah's hometown?

A brief moment in Chicago

I know what you're thinking. No, I didn't visit Oprah on the way in or out of Chicago. She'll have to catch me on the rebound! Tell her people to call my people.

Some time in Las Vegas
Thursday, February 16, 2006

"OK, people! The harder we push, the faster we move!" That's what the man in seat 28C shouted as the plane pulled up to the gate at Las Vegas International Airport. Not the most spiritually correct statement for those of us who pride ourselves on the ability to go with the flow, but I couldn't help smiling anyway.

Now that I'm here in Las Vegas, I have a few days to chill until I head out for Japan.

Why Las Vegas? Well, my friend Ken lives in Las Vegas. You'll recall Ken is the fellow who first told me about Saipan. So I figured I'd make that my last stop before my escape. I've known Ken since 1991 (back in my record label days, he was one of the artists on my label), and I'd never seen his place in "sin city!"

Ken and me in Las Vegas

Passion Prophet composing Friday Life Rhymes in Vegas

Walt in Vegas!

Note 4: Escape From Las Vegas

Saturday, February 18, 2006

After staying with Ken for two days, it's time to leave. So, here's the plan. I'll travel first to Japan, stay there a few days and then continue to Saipan.

By 6:00 a.m., I finally hear back from some of the people I had contacted through friends and through hospitalityclub.org and couchsurfing.com about showing me around while in Japan. These are two unique services through which people all over the world open up their homes (and couches) to let you stay free of cost to make seeing the world a little less impersonal and a whole lot cheaper. My friend David's contact, Yasuko (not her real name), said it was too short notice, and that she had commitments on Monday and Tuesday that would prevent her from hosting me, but that she would be willing to show me around on Sunday afternoon when I arrived. My CouchSurfing.com contact replied that she too, was out of town and wouldn't be able to help me. So, I called up Hotels.com and paid for a one-night reservation at Narita's Mercure Hotel. That would give me a place to stay while I got my bearings, determined the lay of the land and possibly make some other connections and accommodations once in Tokyo.

Things are going great! Excited, I shower, pack and do a final check of my incoming email, and by 7:00 a.m., Ken wakes up, and we prepare to leave for him to drop me off to begin my escape.

Ken and I get to the airport at 8:00 a.m. We stand on line to check in for the 10:00 a.m. American Airlines flight to Tokyo; we get up to the counter, I give Eva the ticket agent my passport and ticket confirmation. She smiles. Yep, things are going great!

Me and Eva. Things are about to take a turn

She looks through my passport.

"Do you have a visa?" she asks.

"Visa!??? Visa??? No one told me I needed a visa??? I think to myself. (Actually, I wasn't really that perturbed. The sense I have of my life being a story to be told is so strong, that I was already starting to compose this episode even as she was telling me this. Ken would later remark that he's seen people kick, scream, curse, throw their luggage and become downright otherworldly when faced with the reality of missing their flight and losing their tickets. For me, it's just another day in Walt World.)

"Yes, sir, you need a visa. As a Jamaican citizen, you need a visa to enter Japan. I can check you in as far as San Jose, but you won't be able to go to Japan."

Well, to make a long story longer, Ken and I go back and forth with her, pleading my case, appealing to her sympathy, asking her to verify the regulations, even asking to speak to a supervisor before finally accepting the finality of her pronouncement.

"So how long does it take to get a visa?" I ask.

"Usually twenty-four hours," she replies.

"Where's the nearest Consulate?" I ask.

"There's one in Los Angeles, and one in San Francisco."

Since Los Angeles is only three hours away, we decide to head there by car on Monday (it's now Saturday), and get everything squared away in time for a Tuesday morning flight. "But wait," I start to think aloud, as I direct the question to Eva, "if I don't make this flight today, will I be able to change it to leave out on Tuesday?"

Eva directs me to the customer service phone

"Sorry, sir, this is a non-refundable fare," she says as she checks her screen. "There'll probably be a fee. You'll have to call Customer Service to find out what that is. You can use the courtesy phone on the wall behind you."

And then it dawns on Ken and me that Monday is President's Day. The Consulate won't be open. That means I would have to get to the Consulate on *Tuesday* and then leave Wednesday.

So we head over to the phones and contact American Airlines customer service where I discover I'll have to pay $900 additional dollars since I'd have to make a new reservation. Now *that's* clearly not an option. (Call me cheap, but I prefer "frugal.")

"Maybe you can go through Hawaii, and then Guam," Ken suggests. "You won't have the visa issue since they're both American territories. Then once you're on Guam, you can always take a boat if you have to to get to Saipan!"

You did say "$900 extra dollars, right?

Pensive prophet ponders paradise particulars

Options are dwindling here, it seems. Ok. Maybe we can change my outbound flight out of Japan to leave the same day. Ken phones Northwest Airlines and starts the holding process.

Meanwhile, I start making calls to American, and then Continental to inquire about flights through Hawaii and discover that they all start at about $1,200. I pull out my laptop and start to search online for fares (luckily the airport was wired). Every airline showed prices of close to $2,000 for a new flight at this time. If, as I always maintain, the universe is perfect and that I'm always guided down the perfect path, then I needed to find that path quickly since time was growing short. So here's the situation: It's now Saturday. I can't get checked in on my flight to Japan without a Visa. I can't get a Visa until Tuesday. But if I change the flight to leave any other day but today, I'll end up paying at least an additional $900. And, if I change the entire route and travel instead via US Territories, I'll essentially have to start the whole booking process from scratch, lose all the existing tickets I've purchased, and that would probably cost at least $1200 to start! Are you following all this?

It's now 9:48 a.m. The flight I'm originally booked on is leaving in twelve minutes, which means it's probably too late to check in and board. I realize that having lost this outbound flight, that it won't be financially possible to get to Japan. If I can't get to Japan, then the Japan to Saipan leg of the trip won't happen. Things are falling apart. I can feel the dream slipping away.

uh-oh...

So now I finally start to sweat. Embarrassing visions of myself getting off the plane back at New York's LaGuardia airport start dancing through my head!

But, in the famous words of my friend, Erroll Paden: *"I ain't goin' out like that!"*

Desperate, not wanting to lose the momentum of this first leg of my journey, I wonder if I should attempt to get on the flight anyway and head to San Jose. Perhaps once I'm at a different airport, I reason, I'll meet with different luck, more knowledgeable agents, or someone who'll just let me through because it's the &%($*%$) right thing to do!!

So I approach the check-in counter once again and wait for Eva to finish helping another passenger. I'm about to jump with no net and simply pray there's water down below.

This time, however, another agent, David S., calls me over.

"Have you guys checked in already?" he asks.

I pause. I wonder if I should keep dealing with Eva or go to David. I decide not to wait for her and start explaining my predicament to David, and then I ask, "Can I still get on the flight to San Jose?" I ask.

"Well, it's too late for that," he says. "They're about to close the boarding gate in five minutes."

"I can run really fast," I offer.

"I don't think that'll matter, "he says with a smile. "It takes twenty minutes just to get to the other side of the terminal where the gates are," he says, as he starts tapping away at this keyboard.

"Here's my original reservation," I show him, continuing to explain my situation as he types.

"Can you contact Northwest and change your reservation to leave the same day you arrive in Japan?" he asks helpfully. "That way you won't need a visa since you won't be leaving the terminal."

"We've been trying," Ken says. "We've been on hold for about forty minutes now."

"Wouldn't it be easier just to go down to the Northwest counter at the end of the terminal?" Dave asks nonchalantly.

Ken and I look at each other and laugh.

Then Dave punches some more keys, and from there at the American Airlines check-in counter, he accesses the Northwest airlines flight schedule and says, "Once you get down there, find out if they can get you on their flight NW77 leaving out of Tokyo on Monday, February 20, then I can change your reservation and put you on a flight to leave tomorrow instead, and that way you can get to Tokyo on the 20th, simply leave later that the same day and not have to worry about the visa issue. You'll essentially only need what's called a Transit Visa. You'll never leave the terminal, and you'll be on your way to Saipan! In fact, here it is," he says handing me my itinerary. "I've already rebooked you on tomorrow's flight."

"You can do that?" I asked. "You can change my reservation to leave tomorrow? And I won't have to pay a change fee, or rebook."

"That's the easy part," he says. (Now why didn't Eva suggest that? I thought silently to myself.) "You just gotta make sure your continuing flight on Northwest can be changed as well so you can make the connection. Go down to the end of the terminal and see if you can make the change."

So Ken and I gather my two pieces of luggage, the laptop, my bag of food, digital camera, and head towards the Northwest ticket counter. After a quick explanation to Judy our agent, she says that flight NW77 leaving out of Japan is all sold out.

"How about stand-by?" I ask. "Can you put me on a stand-by flight?"

"No, I don't think that'll work," she says. "You actually have to show a confirmed continuing flight. They won't accept a stand-by reservation for a Transit Visa."

So Judy wasn't able to make the change. But now that I know that my new best friend, good ol' Dave can work his magic and change my departure date with a few keystrokes, that opens up some new options, I realize that things are going to be all right!

So leaving the Northwest reservation (the one from Japan to Saipan) as it is, Ken and I head back to see Dave at the American Airlines counter, where I ask him to do me another favor.

"Dave," I tell him, "I can't change the original Northwest second leg of the journey, but if you can put me on a Tuesday flight out of here, that will put me in Tokyo for me to connect to the Northwest flight I had originally booked from Tokyo to Saipan. If you can make this happen, Dave," I tell him, "I'll name my first-born son after you."

Before agreeing to the challenge, he reads the regulations to confirm I won't need a visa to enter Saipan, and then he types away for what seems an eternity (making special notations in my reservation so that Tuesday's agent knows the deal) and then voila! I see a crisp new itinerary and flight confirmation shoot out from his printer, and he hands it to me with a smile!

"Dave," I tell him, "I'm writing a book about my little adventures traveling around the world, so this will *definitely* be in it," I say as Ken snaps a picture.

And so it was.

I'm now booked on a flight leaving Las Vegas Tuesday morning, arriving in Tokyo Wednesday afternoon just in time to connect to my original Northwest flight to Saipan! Whew!

Dave's the man!!

I thank him profusely, shake his hand, and we head out. Yes, I'm back in business! Stuck in Las Vegas for two days, but definitely back in business!

*****

It's my philosophy in life that everything happens for a reason. So why has my escape been delayed? Is it because I'll meet someone special on the flight I'm now booked on? Is it to give me more time in the U.S. to take care of some unfinished business? Or perhaps it all happened... just so I could have this story to tell you.

(Thanks to Ken for capturing it all in real time!)

EPILOGUE:

The anatomy of escape. The anatomy of creation.

As I relax after my day of drama at the airport, I'm reading *Ask and it is Given: Learning to Manifest Your Dreams* by Esther and Jerry Hicks. I've just been reminded that I create my own reality. I know this to be true. The challenge, of course, is figuring out the reason for the specific creations that seem out of synch with what one says consciously that one desires to create. I created the escape. I created today's apparent glitch. If so, what was the reason for today's glitch? I must assume that it is of my own creation. Am I sabotaging my escape? Or, am I also creating on other levels of which I am not aware? It's always been my own teachings to my coaching clients that our realities are of our own creation.

I have no one else to blame but myself for failing to fully ascertain the need for a visa for my trip. I know, however, that I will still get to Saipan. I don't believe that there is any other force thwarting my plans. So, I created this apparent delay (unconsciously?) to give myself one more day. Interestingly enough, when I got back to Ken's place, I turned on the radio, found a country music station and shortly heard "One More Day" by Diamond Rio, one of my favorite groups.

Anyway, I can see clearly now that today's events were created by last week's decisions in a moment of indecision. In other words, at some point back when I was making the reservations, when I had ample opportunity to act on the hunch, the information and the awareness that my visa, passport and travel documentation should be in good order, I chose not to. If I think about it, there were times of doubt during the period from when Ken told me about Saipan, and when I actually purchased my tickets to complete the final leg of the journey. I even recall having the opportunity to get the answers I needed and not simply assume that permanent residency was equivalent to US citizenship in that regard. So today was created yesterday. So while I may be committed today; while I may be excited today; while I may be fully ready to create my new life on Saipan, I am living today the effects of yesterday's doubts.

So, what have we learned, boys and girls? Never go to Eva for your boarding pass. No, just kidding. Jamaicans need a visa to go to Japan? Ok, that'll do for now. Lesson learned.

Note 5: Escape from Las Vegas, Take Two!

Tuesday, February 21, 2006
"Right this way, Mr. Goodridge. We've been expecting you."

It's two days later, we're back at the airport, and my now second attempt to escape from Las Vegas is, in a word, effortless. Traffic was cooperative. The doors were all open. There were no lines for check-in. Security check went quickly. The smiles were plentiful, and there was no crowd at the boarding gate. In the famous lyrics of Peter, Paul and Mary: "I'm leaving on a jet plane, don't know when I'll be back again...!" Next stop, San Jose, California for a layover before heading to Japan!

On the flight to San Jose, I meet a young Japanese woman named Yasaka. I share Bob Marley with her. She teaches me how to say a few things in Japanese, including the phrases "I don't eat meat" and "I only eat vegetables." It probably won't come in too handy on the now short layover in Tokyo, but just in case someone grabs me and forces a tuna sandwich on me during customs, I'll be ready! Thanks, Yasaka!

Yasaka listens to "Bob"

My final picture in America taken by Yasaka

I settle in for the ten-hour flight, and contemplate the future...

Hmmmmm. Yes, the future...as in: I wonder if they got my vegetarian meal request right?

Note 6: Escape from Japan!

Wednesday, February 22, 2006

Because of the last-minute flight change I had made thanks to Dave, my request for a veggie meal didn't make it to the new reservation. Not a problem. I learned long ago never to rely on others' concepts of what constitutes vegetarian dining for my sustenance, and being a former boy scout (cub scout, actually), I'm always prepared. I had brought a slew of vegan fruit bars, chips and fruit with me.

Even so, I didn't eat much during the ten-hour flight, just one bar, an apple, and lots of water. The flight attendants were quite helpful and stocked me up with a half-dozen bottles of water during the course of the flight.

"More water, Mr. Goodridge?"

I land in Tokyo's Narita Airport at about 4:50 p.m. local time on February 22. I had about a twenty-minute stay in Japan as I sped through customs to catch my three-hour flight to Saipan!

Welcome to Japan...and Sayonara!
(Hey! Isn't that Yasaka in the lower right?)

Thursday, February 23, 2006

And so it was, beginning with my escape from New York on Wednesday, February 15, enduring:
* a five-hour flight to Las Vegas,

* an aborted escape attempt on February 18, resulting in a total five-day layover in Las Vegas, then,

*a second, this time successful escape attempt on February 21, which included all on the same day:

* a one-hour, twenty minute flight to San Jose, California

* a ten hour flight to Tokyo, Japan,

* a one-hour flight to Nagoya, Japan,

* and a four-hour flight to Saipan, CNMI,

I can finally, on February 23, 2006, end this chapter of my nomadpreneur adventure with the words....

...Welcome to Saipan!

(Just before going through Customs; I stopped a couple to take this, my first picture on Saipan. Thanks, whoever you are!)

Note 7: Welcome to Saipan!

Thursday, February 23, 2006

After clearing customs, I made my way into the warm tropical air, where I was greeted by my host Joe Hill, a successful lawyer on the island, whom Ken had introduced me to by phone back in December 2005. I've since come to learn that Joe is perhaps the most knowledgeable and most qualified person to show me around my new home. Originally from Oklahoma, and an alum of Pepperdine University, Joe has lived all over the US, Alaska and Japan, and has been on the island now for over thirty years. At some point, through both his practice and personality, Joe has come to know practically everyone on the island. (As both testament to his local fame, and perhaps too, the size and culture of the island, he's been known to receive mail from all over the world addressed simply "Joe Hill, Saipan.")

Also there to greet me were Sam Joyner, a well-respected, well-traveled musician, and his brother, John Joyner, recently appointed CNMI Director of Coastal Resources Management.

Joe Hill, Sam Joyner and John Joyner meet me at the airport on Saipan.

Note 8: Where on Earth is Saipan?

I guess now would be an appropriate time to tell you a little bit about Saipan.

Saipan is actually one island of a fourteen-island chain known as the Commonwealth of the Northern Mariana Islands (CNMI). It's about a three-hour flight from Japan; it's about a one-hour flight from Guam. Here on the islands, we refer to ourselves as "the CNMI." After you're here for a while it rolls of your tongue (as in, we here in the *Seen Em Eye*). No one says "NMI," and there are no "Saipanese" anywhere to be found! I've looked!

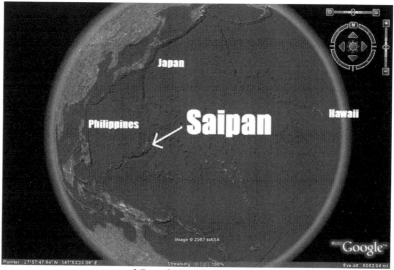

courtesy of Google Earth; labels by Angelo V.

The fourteen volcanic islands in the CNMI are (from north to south): Farallon de Pajaros (aka Uracas), Maug Islands (three islands counted as one), Asuncion, Agrihan, Pagan, Alamagan, Guguan, Sarigan, Anatahan, Farallon de Medinilla, Saipan, Tinian, Aguijan and Rota. They stretch over 375 miles north to south, with a land area of 181 square miles. There are three major inhabited islands, (Saipan, Tinian and Rota) but most live on Saipan.

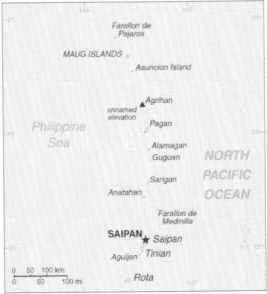

The fourteen islands of the CNMI; courtesy of cia.gov

Saipan is also quite close to the Mariana Trench.

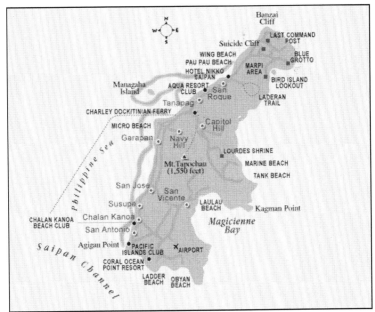

Saipan: The capital of the CNMI

Note 9: Saipan Facts and Figures

CNMI Population: According to latest figures, based on conventional wisdom, the ever-changing population on Saipan is about 60,000. It includes the indigenous Chamorros and Carolinians in addition to contract workers, entrepreneurs, investors, residents, expats, and immigrants from the Philippines, China, Korea, Japan Mainland America, Bangladesh, Canada, Russia, Ghana, Kenya and other countries on the African continent, Thailand, Nepal, Fiji, Chuuk, Pohnpei, Palau, and at least one Jamaican!

CNMI Land mass Size:
Saipan is about 12.5 miles long and 5.5 miles wide
Saipan's total land area is 120 sq km or 46.5 square miles

To put that in perspective:
- Saipan is about the size of San Francisco.
- Saipan is larger than Hong Kong but smaller than Washington, DC.
- Saipan is smaller than Barbados
- All 14 islands of the CNMI combined just equal the size of Barbados
- Manhattan, at 59.5 sq km (23 sq mi), is half the size of Saipan
- Staten Island, at 151.5 sq km (58.5 sq mi) is a little larger than Saipan
- The Bronx, at 109 sq km (42 sq mi) is a little smaller than Saipan
- Queens, at 282.9 sq km (109.2 sq mi), is a bit more than twice Saipan
- Brooklyn, at182.9 sq km (70.6 sq mi) is 1.5 times Saipan's size
- Brooklyn has 2.5 million people compared to Saipan's 66,000
- Jamaica's land area is 4,411 square miles, 95 times Saipan's size!

History and Colonial Influence:
The Spanish were the first Europeans to encounter the Chamorro and occupied these islands from 1600-1898.
German rule began in 1899 and lasted until 1914, when the Japanese took over the island under a League of Nations mandate.
On June 15, 1944, during World War II, U.S. Marines landed on Saipan and fought to secure it from the Japanese. A covenant to establish a commonwealth in political union with the US was approved in 1975, and came into force on March 24, 1976.

Culture: As a result of these colonial influences, the current culture is a hybrid of indigenous Chamorro and Carolinian, plus Spanish, German, Japanese and American influences.

Relationship to US:
The CNMI is a commonwealth in relationship with the United States. It is self-governing, with it's own tax collection and immigration laws. In addition,
- the CNMI is on the US dollar and US Postal system
- those born in the CNMI are US citizens
- the CNMI is considered "outside" of the US (an important piece of information for US permanent resident/green card holders)*

Getting here:
Most US residents flying to Saipan will likely go first to Japan, then directly to Saipan, or from Japan→Guam→Saipan. It's also possible to get here via Hawaii→Guam→Saipan.
Russians flying here can take the Moscow→Shanghai→Saipan route or through direct charter flights.
Chinese flying here can come via China→Korea→Japan→Saipan, or China→Japan→Saipan.
Koreans fly direct from Incheon or Busan.
Japanese may fly from Osaka, Tokyo or Nagoya.
Airlines serving the CNM, their routes and flights are always changing, given the economic conditions at the time of this writing, but at present the carriers which actually land on Saipan are Northwest, Asiana, Freedom Air, and Cape Air.

Topography of note:
Mount Tapochau, at 1,554 feet is the highest point. The measurement from the floor of the Marianas Trench to the crest of Tapochau is 37,752 feet or 7.15 statute miles, (from sea level Mount Everest measures <u>only</u> 29,028 feet). Saipan's 54-mile coast line is irregular except on the western side where there is a fringing reef. A large part of the island is public land.
If you're curious to find out other visit facts, visit http://www.cnmi-guide.com/info/main.html
https://www.cia.gov/cia/publications/factbook/print/cq.html (some info on these sites is a bit outdated, so just keep reading *Jamaican on Saipan* for the real deal!

Some of this immigration and travel information is expected to change as the Department of Homeland Security implements US Immigration laws on the Commonwealth on November 28, 2009. Check out my website www.destinationsaipan.com for details and updates.

Note 10: Off to a Great Start!

The night I landed on Saipan, Joe Hill and I stayed up talking until about three in the morning. After a short sleep, we were up and about to see the island. First stop, Joe Hill's Law Offices!

You can find Joe's offices in Susupe behind Shirley's coffee shop.

After the first of what would be many mini-tours of the island, replete with history and culture lessons, I found myself pulling up to one of the government offices on the island. Joe and the members of the African American Cultural Preservation Committee had been hard at work publicizing my arrival.

And so it came to be that within forty-eight hours of landing on the island of Saipan, I was meeting with Senator Maria Pangelinan and Representative Cinta Kaipat, and finalizing plans for a Passion Profit workshop while here on Saipan.

A workshop is tentatively scheduled for March 11!

Congresswoman Cinta Kaipat & Senator Maria Pangelinan

Jamaican On Saipan! 39

Joe Hill, Rep. Cinta Kaipat, Sen. Maria Pangelinan and me

Senator Pangelinan has the distinction of being the first female senator on Saipan. Representative Kaipat has a distinguished history of public service. Both have been active advocates of the rights and freedoms of Saipan's indigenous and transplanted citizenry.

A few days later, I appeared on KZMI-FM radio to promote the event.

Promoting the workshop on Harry Blaylock's "Island Issues" morning talk show. Shown: Joe, Tony Cabrera, me, Harry.

Note 11: First Impressions

Sunday, March 05, 2006

Despite what my business suits, engineering degree, list of author credits and other accomplishments may indicate to the contrary, I'm really just an Old Harbour, Jamaican country boy at the core. So my first morning on Saipan when I was greeted with the sound of roosters crowing, I smiled a very wide smile.

Of course, this photo loses something in black and white...

The landscape of Saipan is a lot like Jamaica. There are mountains always visible, fruit trees, and hibiscus flowers.

You don't have to go far to experience the rural. The island is small enough that a single turn off the main road can instantly transport you into a more rustic, rural landscape. Where I'm staying right now is more like a home in the country. Untamed bush, swaying coconut trees, chickens, cows and birds within eye and earshot. If I were in Jamaica, this would be more similar to where I lived with my maternal grandparents in Old Harbor. And yet, less than a mile away is Beach Road, where I can find Louis Vitton at the Galleria Mall, and tearooms offering $3,000 bottles of wine.

Practically every place on Saipan is wired! Every hotel lobby, restaurant and coffee shop is set up with wireless internet access. Even the car dealership has Internet access! Every place you can sit, you can surf! And in most cases it's free! Of course, you might feel a little guilty sitting in a coffee shop using the wireless access without at least purchasing a cup of tea or coffee, so at the very least, your access may cost a few dollars.

The ubiquity of wireless Internet access is a welcome surprise. It makes doing the nomadpreneur thing so much easier.

The sign I'm pointing to says "Wireless Internet Available here...FREE... Bring Your Laptop!"

And you're never more than five minutes from the water!

First of many gratuitous beach scenes to remind you where I am! Saipan!

My "tour guide," Joe Hill, has taken me around the island (in style),

..introduced me to government officials, and business owners.

Irene, a local beauty salon owner

Joe Ayuyu (pronounced Azuzu) is the owner of the first McDonald's restaurant on the island. (No, I didn't tell him I'm vegan.)

...organized a "Meet Walt" event at Wild Bill's Bar & Grill to introduce me to the residents,

A preview of things to come

Educated me on Saipan's history...

WWII Japanese tanks at the Last Command Post

...introduced me to long-time residents on the island...

Herb Soll and Joe go way back. It was at Herb's suggestion that Joe ended up on Saipan in the 1970s. Joe's plan was to stay three years at most.

..and shown me the beauty of the island

The view from Banzai Cliff at the north end of the island

Student performers rehearsing at the Fiesta Hotel

And I've still got time to enjoy the rainbows...

Rainbow from my room window at Joe's house; ....(if you're reading this in paperback, trust me, there's one there!)

...walk along Beach Road and do some work in the shade of the pavilions along the path....

Me and my Mac

ahhhhhhhh, yes....

Did I mention I love sunshine? The range of temperatures here on Saipan is from about 83° F at night to 93° F during the day. Perfect!

Note 12: Sights and Sounds Only a Jamaican Can Truly Appreciate.

There's a unique sense of pride that only a Jamaican can appreciate when, upon arriving in a foreign land 8,730 miles away from home, you hear your country's music blasting on stereos, and playing on radio and in clubs. (I have a video I posted on YouTube of me driving around Saipan with the roots band Natural Ites' "Picture on the Wall" playing in the background). Or when you see Bob's face on t-shirts and pickup trucks. Sure, Bob is an iconic world figure, but he is and always will be "our" Bob.

Those of us who grew up in New York during the 70s remember when, if you heard Reggae blaring, it could only be a Jamaican. That soon changed as African Americans, Dominicans, Hatians, and everybody else caught on. These days, here in the Pacific, the person blasting Burning Spear's Christopher Columbus could be Chamorro, Carolinian, Chuukese, Hawaiian, or from Yap. Yep, it's a nice feeling!

"You a go tired fi see me face!"—Bob. (We call him simply 'Bob.')

Normally, I wouldn't call attention to the misspellings of the English language you sometimes find on this side of the world, but this one, at least for a Jamaican, is worth an extra look!

"RASTAurant? Does that mean they serve Ital food?"*

*"Simiya**! A Saipan mi deh!"*

*Ital or I-tal is food often celebrated by those in the Rastafari movement. The word derives from the English word "vital", with the initial syllable replaced by i.[1] This is done to many words in the Rastafari vocabulary to signify the unity of the speaker with all of nature.[Wiki]

*In Jamaican patois, if someone says "Si mi ya," they are saying "See Me Here," as in "here I am!" Here on Saipan, it's the Chamorro word for 'seed.'

Practically all the fruits I grew up with in Jamaica are here on Saipan. There are mangoes, breadfruit, papaya, sweetsop, soursop, naseberry (sapodilla, *chico* here on Saipan), star apple, Otaheite apple, jackfruit, coconut, pineapple! I once said that the only thing I DIDN'T see here was ackee, and Jimbilin (a small yellow/white, sour-tasting cherry-sized fruit). Well, last week, while interviewing Willie Brundidge, Jr. at his home for a Tribune article, I found it!!! Jimbilin!!!

Speaking of sounds, someone needs to re-program these roosters. They crow <u>constantly</u> throughout the day and night. I grew up thinking that a roosters mission was to herald the break of day, but perhaps these guys here are serving a different purpose. I've heard that there are over a dozen different ethnicities and nationalities on the island, so maybe they're programmed for all the different time zones represented on Saipan!

Simiya inna di Jimbilin tree!

There goes another one! And it's 12:17 in the afternoon! It's really not a bother to me personally. I hardly notice it, and when I do, it's just a pleasant reminder that I'm not in New York. As I sit here writing, the only sounds are the constant rustle of leaves in the breeze, birds chirping, the very distant sounds of a car, chickens clucking, and those roosters!

Note 13: Passion Prophet in Paradise!

The Passion Profit workshop that Joe Hill, Senator Pangelinan and Congresswoman Kaipat organized took place! It was fantastic! About seventy people showed up! There were business owners, students, and the passion-minded from various and sundry backgrounds.

During the workshop, local musician, producer, and teacher Sam Joyner proposed that we have an informal Sunday gathering to offer participants the follow-up, follow-through and support most people need after being introduced to a new way of thinking. I was invited to help kick off the Unofficial Saipanpreneur Network. The next day, Sunday, at 3 p.m. at local watering hole

Wild Bill's on Beach Road, we met, brainstormed, shared insights and got working on a few projects that will shortly see the light of day! Some of the projects, websites and products started at that first meeting are still active three years later.

A few weeks later, at the request of Dr. John Joyner, I did a workshop for CRM (Department of Coastal Resources Management)

After that, I conducted a brief, in-house visit and chat at WIA --The Workforce Investment Agency,

and finally, a *Turn Your Passion into Online Profits* workshop at the Northern Marianas College.

Note 14: Meeting the Governor

Monday, March 13, 2006

    I just had a meeting with Governor Benigno Fitial and his entire cabinet! The week prior, I was told I would get to sit in on a cabinet meeting sometime during the day the coming Monday. But it seems there was a bit of a miscommunication, because when I called my contact person in the cabinet, John Joyner (Director of Coastal Resource Management) at 8:30 a.m., I was told the meeting was about to start and that I needed to be there right away!

    So here I was, dressed in shorts, an unpressed shirt, sandals and a bad haircut about to meet with everyone of political significance on Saipan. So I rushed home, switched into more appropriate clothes, then rushed out. When I got to the Governor's offices on Capital Hill, John told me I wasn't just going to sit in, but that since what I had to offer might benefit the most pressing concern of the administration at the time (forced reduction of work hours for several thousand government employees), I was actually going to kick off the meeting, and that everyone was waiting.

    So with about twenty seconds to prepare, (my sales came in handy!) I soon found myself doing my sting how we could interpret the forced work reduction as a "golden opportunity" to focus on turning one's passion into profit.

    I tell you I was in the zone, man!! It was, in my estimation, one of the better four-minute impromptu speeches I've given! I got cool feedback from the acting Minister of Finance who joked that he wanted to send me a list tonight of all the people who would be affected as well as the retirees so I could help them out!

Note 15: Elements of Fame (email break)

An ongoing high point of my time here in the CNMI has been keeping in touch with my friends back in the states via email updates on the happenings here. Answering the types of questions my friends and relatives have been asking has afforded me the opportunity to reflect and analyze myself, my dreams and my feelings. This is from an email I sent to Joe Hill, John Joyner, Sam Joyner, Ken and my buddy Ernest back in NY.

hey Joe, John, Sam, Ken, Ernest

Just want to say thanks for making my dreams come true! As you may know, as part of a marketing/publicity campaign, I set a goal for myself back in October of last year to achieve a certain degree of exposure for my passion-profit philosophy and products. I announced the challenge on my "Elements of Fame" blog. (That was before I had even heard of Saipan.)

Well, as things often happen in this creative universe of ours, forces conspired to bring to me my dreams. Sixty days after setting that goal, Ken introduced me to Saipan. Roughly 50 days after that I'm on a plane executing my escape from America!

Now that I am here on Saipan, the Elements of Fame timeline has sped up considerably. Here's a recap:

- I landed on Saipan on Thursday February 23rd, 2006

- 1 day later on Friday, February 24, 2006 I was speaking to a Senator and a congresswoman about a workshop

- 8 days after landing, on Friday March 3, 2006, I was featured in the *Saipan Tribune* and the *Marianas Variety*, the two leading English-language papers on the island.

- 10 days after landing, on Sunday March 5, 2006, I was again in the *Tribune's* Sunday edition

- 11 days after landing, on Monday March 6, 2006 I was on Harry Blaylock's radio show which aired several times during the week.

- 16 days after landing, on Saturday, March 11, 2006 I was doing my first workshop on island.

- 18 days after landing, on Monday, March 13, 2006 I was addressing the Governor & his cabinet

- 22 days after landing, on Friday, March 17, 2006 I was doing a workshop for CRM, which was filmed by KMCV television and for which I was interviewed,

- 25 days after landing, just last night on Monday, March 20, 2006 I was featured on the KMCV 6 p.m. evening news (This airs at 6 p.m., then at 10 p.m. and the next day at 6:30 a.m. and noon)

So, in less than thirty days after landing in the CMNI (That's what WE call the Commonwealth of the North Mariana Islands here), I was in featured in print, on radio and on television in the country's major media outlets, met with senators, congresswomen and other cabinet members, I'm selling books, securing coaching clients and being invited to local political and social events, making new friends while surrounded by friendly people, warm weather, and, ahem...some very beautiful "scenery!"

Thanks, gentlemen, for your individual efforts and contributions to this worthy cause: my happiness! ☺

Can't wait to see what happens next! I'll keep you posted.
Walt [end of email]

Yet another gratuitous beach scene to remind you where I am: Saipan!

Note 16: Alien Soul (email break)

Hi Walt,
Hard for it to sink in that you're half way cross the world. Do you still feel like a tourist or are you beginning to feel like a long term visitor? —Chris

Interesting question. Thanks for asking it. But I don't think those are the right choices or options for how I feel...Let me think for a minute. I may have been a visitor, but I'm NEVER a tourist!! The word "tourist" has negative connotations for me, you know. Must be a Jamaican thing. I think the operative words for me around this topic are really:

Alien, Adventure, Adapt, and Adjust

Ever since coming to America in the seventies, I've always felt like an alien, an outsider, an observer waiting for the day to come when I returned "home." So every experience outside of Jamaica, West Indies has always been "time away from home" for me. As a result, there's a restlessness that pervades everything I do, and everywhere I rest, since I always perceive myself to be not just an alien, but an alien on a mission.

That mission, that sense of calling, that desire to be, do and have something specific happen in my life is what prompted my departure from the Port Authority, the launch of the record label, the experience with ACN (American Communications Network), the move to Maryland, the book writing, the speaking engagements, and everything else about my entrepreneurial yearnings. Unless and until I feel that I've reached some level of significant accomplishment (I'm aware that it's the nature of such yearnings, that their attainment is inherently and necessarily elusive), I never really expect to feel at home anywhere I go. Everything is transient while I'm on this mission and journey.

Therefore, I think I would define how I feel as that of being on an adventure—a quest to find a comfortable place where I can live my veggie lifestyle while fulfilling my purpose, achieving the recognition and widespread reach I desire, interacting with cool people and having fulfilling romantic experiences. Every place I've lived, therefore, has been an adventure where I *adapt and adjust* to the environment and the circumstances at hand while constructing elements of, and "cracking the code" for the dream that drives me. Adaptation and adjustment are easy in that context for everything (every benefit and every burden) is "just for a while."

Every time I get a new apartment, move to a new city, launch a new marketing campaign, or even start a new relationship, it's with the tacit understanding that this is a momentary thing. It's part of a bigger vision. I know there may come a time when I'll need to move on. Everything but the dream-goal is just the adventure of the moment. Unless things are just right, there's no reason to get comfortable...there's a voice in my head that says "you've got a goal to accomplish, goshdarnit!!" (You'll notice my inner voice often as a corny, politically correct way of communicating, and like me, doesn't curse.)

Now, however, we're in a different ballgame! Things have shifted. As I've said before, visually, Saipan is just like Jamaica. The rhythm of the people is different, but the pace of life is about the same. There's reggae playing constantly, mango, breadfruit, and coconut trees line the streets. Were it not for the fact that there are all these Micronesian and Asian people walking about, I could easily believe that I was in "JA."

Furthermore, what makes this a different experience is that it's the first place I've lived that has so many of the elements of the dream that drives me. I've got the Jamaica-esque landscape. I've got the beauty. I've got the sun and warmth. And, unlike any other period of time before, I've got the fame, respect and notoriety and the real ability to affect change in a society in a significant way. With only 60,000 people on the island, an appearance on national television, meetings with the Governor and all that I mentioned in my previous email, have more significance. Everything else that the island DOESN'T have (vegan stores, my kind of health-consciousness) are all things that can be worked on or around, and in fact, present new business ideas.

My friend Ken asked me recently if I regret making the decision to come here. The way I see it, the mindset of a true nomad is such that there's no such thing as regret. There is only "here" and "not here." If "here" is unpleasant, then any step forward is better than "here." Once you get to a new "here," if it is not to your liking, there's always another step forward you can take. So, there are never regrets, just the decision to stay or go. But what I do know is that right now I feel like the happiest man alive! Here's what I told Ken:

- First of all, just being able to say "I live on the island of Saipan in the Pacific" is worth the price of admission!

- It's like being transported back into time to the way Jamaica was when I left it, and probably more like it was in the 60's. It's relatively safe, scenic and still relatively untainted by certain western ways.

-It has a small town feel, which I didn't realize I liked so much. I can remember people's names after meeting them the first time. (Haven't been able to do that since 1st grade in Jamaica)

- The challenge of achieving a certain degree of publicity in 365 days that I set for myself is coming true here on Saipan.

- Within one day of landing, I was talking with Senators and Congresswomen. Within six days I was on the radio. Within eight days my face was plastered within a half-page spread in the leading newspaper. Within nine days, I was addressing the Governor of the island and his entire cabinet! (see previous email)

- I've been having some wonderful experiences. And I'm learning new languages at the same time.

- Healthwise: I get to sweat all day, which because of my fanatic health focus is a good way to keep toxin-free. I get access to fresh fruits and vegetables all throughout the island.

Even my minimalism has been kicked up a notch and I'm not even thinking about my records and the stuff in my apartment.

Every day here the dream just gets better and better. I can't even begin to describe how tickled I am driving around the roads, seeing the ocean all around, experiencing the friendliness of the people and knowing that the next phone call I get is probably an invitation to have a new experience that will allow me to live more of the dream. It feels like I'm coasting. All the tension and stress of the last ten years of sowing seeds has been lifted. It's now feeling like harvest time.

So, I say all of that to say this: the move to Saipan is part of a continuing adventure. While it has 90% of what I've been looking for, I'm not naive enough to say that this is where the journey ends. There's always a bigger vision. Who knows? The continuing saga may include Africa, China, Australia, Antarctica, back to America or wherever!

So am I a visitor? a tourist? We're all visitors here (on this plane, and on the planet). "Long-term" is a relative concept depending on how you experience time. Tourist implies having a place to return...no such thing for a nomad. But I could ramble on for hours, so I'll leave you with this to wrap up.

Life is the "visit", and time is on loan
And dreamers move on like the famed rolling stone
A nomad, by nature finds new lands to roam
And an alien, though happy, is never at home

Your friend, Walt "the happy alien" *[end of email]*

Note 17: Let the Music Play
March 28, 2006

hi, *[a private email sent to a few close friends and family]* just some early morning thoughts I felt like sharing:

There are times, early in the morning, as I lie awake in bed listening to the radio here on Saipan, that my life takes on an almost surreal quality. It's now 3:17 a.m. on Tuesday morning, March 28, 2006. It's my favorite time of day. Things are quiet. I'm listening to 103.9FM, (sort of a Lite-FM-type format) and just heard "Dancing Queen" by Abba, followed by "Sharing the Night Together" by Dr. Hook, and "Let's Get it On" by Marvin Gaye. A few days ago I heard "Kung Fu Fighting" by Carl Douglas. Now, if you're not familiar with those songs, they are big 70's and early 80's hits. What's significant about those songs in particular is that they're from a period in the 70's and 80's that corresponds to my best memories of life in Jamaica before I moved to the states, and during the summers when, homesick, I would go back to visit.

Like a lot of people, music has always been a special marker of moments. They are life's soundtrack capable of eliciting memories of moments lived. When I hear those songs, I'm immediately transported to those early innocent times of my life and feel nostalgia mixed with an indescribable peace and contentment that makes me almost cry. ("That's the Time I Feel Like Making Love" by Roberta Flack, "Loving You" by Minnie Ripperton and "Rock the Boat" by the Hues Corporation are three songs in particular that have that effect on me).

So here I am, many years later, living once again in a tropical paradise that has the Jamaica-style feel of back in the 70s, eating the same fruits that grow there, meeting nice people with the same nomadic/adventurer streak, surrounded by native beauty, and experiencing the career fulfillment, and acceptance on the level I have dreamt of and strived all my life to create.

So when I hear these songs in this my new dream life, time slows down, and it's like I've been given another chance to pick up and continue my life where I've always felt like it was halted. And when I hear any other songs from my past, they too feel different. They're being reprogrammed into new memories, synchronized with a new set of feelings and becoming the soundtrack of this my new life's adventure.

They say you can't go back. "They" would be wrong, indeed. But I've even done one better: I've gone back and taken my dreams with me. I wish everyone the singular experience and joy of finding the dream that feeds them and of getting the chance to live it on their own terms.

Let the music play.

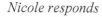
Nicole responds

Wow, Walt. I really appreciate you sharing those thoughts with me. I can feel the "passion" of your experiences. I feel like I'm there....well, a little (since, after reading your emails, reality sets in when I can't feel the warmth of the sun or walk around half-naked).... but every time you speak about the peacefulness and natural ambience of Saipan, it reminds me of how I felt when I took my own trip to Jamaica. I have yet to relive that experience. This email made me feel sentimental.

I'm really proud of you and so glad you're living out your dreams. I'm sure you're in heaven. Next, the glass house. Will it be in Jamaica? You should put all of these thoughts in your memoir. Hmmmm, "Quiet Time With Walt." You *are* going to write one, aren't you? I'm sure you're ahead of me on that. I really like this part of your email:

> "So when I hear these songs in this my new dream life, time slows down, and it's like I've been given another chance to pick up and continue my life where I've always felt like it was halted. And when I hear any other songs from my past, they too feel different. They're being reprogrammed into new memories, synchronized with a new set of feelings and becoming the soundtrack of this my new life's adventure.
>
> They say you can't go back. "They" would be wrong, indeed. But I've even done one better: I've gone back and taken my dreams with me."

Enjoy living out your dreams, Walt.
Have a Blessed and Prosperous Day, Nicole

---

* My Glass House. My friends know that one of my dreams is to have a completely glass house like one I saw featured in Dwell Magazine. However, Saipan is such a small town, I may have to forego this particular dream for the sake of modesty. People will see more than I may wish!

My friend, Nava, responds

I feel you more than you know, I too have those moments when I hear an old song from the 70's or 80's and I am transported into a time and place where it was sweet, it brings me to happy tears, I begin to smell and taste things that were around at that time, and have a real clear visual of that particular period when I too was happy and safe and carefree and dancing like a child and didn't care who was watching (but of course they were, because I am such a great dancer by nature). And what do you mean do I know these songs? Abba's "Dancing Queen" was my theme song :-) A few weeks back I was to meet a friend of mine at 3'oclock and I was late because I was listening to Hal Jackson's Sunday morning Classics show and one of my favorite Lou Rawls songs "I'll See You When You Get There," was playing and it immediately thrust me back to a time I was going through a break up and make up and that was our reunited song. When I arrived 15 minutes late, my friend apologized to me because he too was late because he, like myself, was listening to Hal Jackson's show and couldn't walk out the house until he danced as I did! He said "[darn] she'll see me when I get there!" When I told him I was doing the same thing, we just hugged each other and said at the same time it was a moment we could not miss. We didn't then when we were younger, and would not allow ourselves to miss that moment again now. So on my birthday I received a CD of Lou Rawls Favorite Love Songs and, of course, that song was on the CD, so I can elicit that memory at any moment I choose. I live for my "Deja vu Mojo Reminiscing Moments!" I could not live this life without them and can't wait to experience and make more memorial moments.

I am so glad you have a radio station that plays all the old jams and takes you to those happy safe places. If I was stranded on an island and I could take one thing with me it would be my music from the 70's and 80's. May the music always comfort you. Peace, Love, Nava

My friend Derek responds:

Hey Walt, Thanks for sharing your thoughts. I can definitely appreciate the transference that takes place when listening to music that takes me to a nostalgic place. For me it was also Jamaica........Queens that is! "Funkin' for Jamaica" is a song that brings me back home. I've been collecting classic R&B for years until it became more available in other formats like CDs and now MP3. I can think of many songs that bring me close to tears as well. There are songs like "Check it Out", "Natural High", and "A Million Dollars" that I can play over and over without tiring. *end of email]*

My Aunt Flo ("Jim" to the family), living in Jamaica, responds:

My Dear Nephew;
Thanks. Absolute delight getting this email from you!
You have summed up exactly why I play mostly 'old' music on my programmes here in Jamaica. Given the drastic changes which have gone on in our country - which is not unique, thanks to American cultural imperialism -I find that it eases the stress and confusion being expressed by some callers by using the music to remind them of happier times, or that problems have always existed,

As part of the desire is to use the programme to 'teach' in an unobtrusive way, my greatest disappointment is that I am unable to find Negro Spirituals. Well do I remember on Friday nights how the family, with Mother or Brother Ben playing the piano, would sing together "Swing Low Sweet Chariot" and others. Mother would explain the significance of the words and the role of the music in the liberation movement to us then we would sing each song again with feeling.

Good Lord! I haven't heard "Kung Fu Fighting" in years. Must see if the Record Library has a copy. I am studiously ignoring your comment re me and 'knowing' the music! Don't you know I am the disappointment of the family when it comes to music? My musical ability expressed itself through my dancing ability despite the serious knuckle licks I used to get from a frustrated elder brother, my feet are (were?) my musical instrument.

You are indeed fortunate that you are able to live your dream. Enjoy for yourself and for all those who for a variety of reasons have been denied the opportunity/or have not had the nerve to take the plunge required to make their dreams reality.
Nuff Love. Guidance and Protection.
Aunt Jim. [Florizelle O'Connor]

Howard responds:

Aahhhhhhhhhhh!

The sigh of relief and joy resulting from an exhilarating moment. I sure do enjoy hearing of your experiences there on Saipan.

Yes, the joy and the peace you feel can be the experience of your soul back on its path; back in the groove so to speak, bringing forth past memories of bliss, allowing you to associate your current experience with that which is good for you/soul. You have been sufficiently open to risk and free of attachments (minimalist) to have found your way back into synchronous vibration with your soul.

This current state may be the source for the great adept to come forth. What diet germane to soul will sustain the synchrony?

You may currently be open, to an even deeper connection with soul. This may require going inward. This inward passage may occur through stillness meditation or through an instantaneous transcendental experience. See how you are led. There may be a guide there on the island waiting for you. At the very least, be sure to spend copious amounts of time very close to nature as the Earth Mother is conscious of your growth and needs.

Aaaahhhhhhhhhhhhh
Namaste
Howard

Howard, a fellow Jamaican, is one of those people everyone needs as a friend. He must have been writer, sage, guru, in all of his previous and current lives. His are the types of emails that you look forward to reading. Unfortunately I can't share the best of them here as they contain words like "succulent", "fatted calves", "hyper-satisfaction", "pleasure-induced sanpaku" etc...

But, who knows, as Howard himself has said: "Walt, I have noted what appears to be a chapter missing from your journal. You did not mention any exploits with the long and lean 'Susan.' But, I expect, in years to come there will be that which becomes known as 'The Long Lost Chapters'" :o)

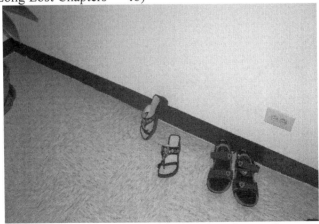

A preview, perhaps of the long lost chapters?

Note 18: The Most Important Day of My Life

April 1, 2006

Hello my dearest friends...from Walt.

Little did I realize when I left the house this morning that this would turn out to be the single, most impactful, significant and life-altering day of my life. Something happened to me of great and profound meaning, and I had to share it with you my dearest friends.

Everything else I've documented up to today pales in comparison to what I'm about to share with you.

Yes, I've picked up and "left" America; yes, I've met with senators and congresswomen; yes, I've met with the governor--the highest elected official on the island--and his cabinet; yes, I've been on radio, featured in newspapers, and on national television; yes, I'm recognized on the street and have more offers for speaking engagements and coaching clients than I know what to do with; and yes, I'm having a wonderful time socially, But today, my friends, what happened today tops them all!!! And what is it, you ask, that has shaken my world to its very foundation and has me doing cartwheels up and down the one paved road here on Saipan? I can sum it up in three words...

Health Valley® Cookies.

That's right!!! Health Valley Cookies! I've found them! They're here! While strolling down the aisle in a local supermarket, I found a box of cookies I can actually eat!!! Now they're not Cindy's Raw cookies from Health Nuts in NY, or the carob spirulina bars from the Food Co-op in Brooklyn. But they're wheat-free, dairy free, and juice-sweetened, and the closest thing to my kind of treat I've found since I've been here!

Now that may not seem like much to some of you—those of you whose dietary choices allow you to include Oreos, Nilla Wafers and Fig Newtons in your daily fare—but those of us who are vegan, and who shun white flour, eggs, sugar, milk, butter and artificial sweeteners, have a hard enough time finding consumable selections even in cities like New York.

Now I haven't made a big deal about the dietary selection here on the island, but everything here's got sugar, monosodium glutamate, (and did I mention sugar?) in it So, I had essentially resigned myself to going completely without my usual treats to feed my own natural/organic) sweet tooth. But not any more, my friends. Not any more! My world as changed. And it's all because of, everyone say it with me now: HEALTH VALLEY COOKIES.... (the words bring tears to my eyes...>sniff<)

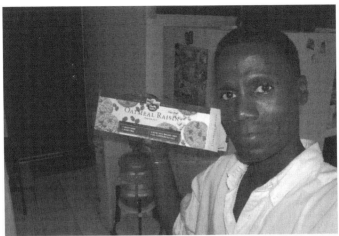

Here's a picture I just took to commemorate this MAJOR event.

Oh, yeah...almost forgot: Met a nice young lady from Thailand. Had a nice time....yadda, yadda, yadda...
But getting back to the important stuff....
ahem...Health Valley Cooooookies.......ahhhhhhhh!

Note 18: Vegan in Paradise

So since we're on the topic of food, let me share what it's like being vegan in paradise.
Now far be it for me to come 7,778 miles across the seas to live in a new land and disparage the dietary choices of the local population. That would be insensitive, presumptuous and rude of me. I will say, however, that my own choice not to eat meat—I've been vegan since 1992—and my staying away from processed food, makes finding fare to suit my tastes a bit of a challenge here. But even life-long Saipan residents see the sad irony in the direction of the island's dietary norms. To illustrate, I'll simply show you the bumper sticker on the back left window of this van.

66   Jamaican On Saipan!

Yes, that's right, it says "I Love SPAM" not as in unsolicited email, but as in Hormel's mystery meat Spam. We don't see too many of these bumper stickers stateside.

Random, gratuitous beach scene to remind you where I am! Saipan!

Note 20: The Saipan Tribune

April 4, 2006
    As I became more familiar with the economic situation here in the CNMI, I decided there was something I could do to help. I submitted a proposal to the two major English-language newspapers on the island suggesting a *"weekly column entitled "THE SAIPANPRENEUR PROJECT" featuring passionpreneur profiles, business tips, book excerpts and unique inspiration. The goal of The Saipanpreneur Project Column is to help revitalize the economy by stimulating entrepreneurial thought and activity within the population of the CNMI."*
    I received an email from Jayvee Vallejera, the editor of the *Saipan Tribune* two days later, met with him the day after that, and we made it official. So on Wednesday, April 12, 2006, the first installment of my Saipanpreneur Project column appeared in the *Saipan Tribune*. Since then, my articles have been appearing weekly in the *Tribune*. The preamble of each article states:

The only way to take control of your life, raise your standard of living and move beyond merely surviving is to create your own unique product or service that you offer to increasing numbers of people in exchange for the things of value that you desire. This simple formula applies to countries as well as people. A self-sufficient economy has its own products or services of value to export to the world. Similarly, a self-sufficient individual has something of value to exchange in the global marketplace. That thing of value is based on your natural talent, skill, or interest—in other words, your passion!
    I've had the pleasure of meeting some unique Saipanpreneurs, helping them succeed by giving them some exposure in the press, and getting people talking about new ideas. The archives are available at www.saipantribune.com (search for "walt goodridge") or on my Walt's Escape from America Blog at www.passionprofit.com/escape

Saipanpreneur landscaper: Willie Brundidge, Jr. (center) of Mozell's Boys Landscaping

Saipanpreneur filmmakers Ben and Dan of the Looking for America DVD (see Saipanpreneur.com)

Saipanpreneur crafters Daniel D. and Remy Babauta and Daniel's coconut handicrafts (see Saipancrafts.com)

Note 21: Martin Luther King Day Legislation Passed!

Big news! On Tuesday, April 12, 2006, the governor signed into law a bill proclaiming Martin Luther King Jr's birthday as a legal holiday in the CNMI.

That's Cinta Kaipat seated next to Governor Fitial. The bill was the first legislation she got passed!

Some of those within the community who made it all possible!

Note 22: Sistah Constable
May 1, 2006

A little known fact outside of Saipan is that the Assistant Attorney General for Saipan is a woman by the name of Rebecca Warfield, a "sistah" from Mississipi.

Rebecca Warfield, from Mississippi to Micronesia

Her husband is Jeff Warfield, the chief prosecuting attorney.

Jeff Warfield

Since taking that photo, and within the year I was here, Rebecca was appointed to the position of Commissioner of Public Safety! Yep, there's a new sheriff in town!

Note 23: Settling in

I started learning Mandarin Chinese officially yesterday. Attended another get-together of the brothas and sistahs on the island, plus a birthday party.

That's Sam Joyner doing the DJing honors

Me and friend Ben at a family gathering

I went sailing.

Attended the Flame Tree Arts Festival, an annual event where dozens of vendors come out to sell arts, crafts, food and more!

That's Tim and Adelia San Nicholas of Rota who flew over to Saipan to sell their Daok oil at the Flame Tree Festival.

A few days later, I was invited to Kagman High School, (there are 10 elementary, and 2 Jr. high schools on island)—to judge the poetry, performance and presentation skills of students for the regional Forensics League Competition.

The judges. That's me on the far right, second from the end, just in case you have trouble finding me.

Trench Wars!

Went to see "Trench Wars!" That's an extreme fighting, Mixed Martial Arts event where competitors in a cage use any means possible to basically end normal brain activity and the bodily functions of their opponents.

Oh, the savagery! The blood! The mayhem, the carnage, the raw, untamed brutality of it all! And all for only twenty bucks!

Moved into my new apartment on the 25th of April.

Note 24: New York Calling...

Dear Walt:
Your Aunt Nye will be celebrating her 80th birthday on July 3rd this year. Her grandchildren are planning a family birthday bash for her on June 29th. I just spoke to your Dad in New York about his attendance. He is not sure he will be going as "Walt is not here to travel with him." Do you think you could leave Paradise for a few days to facilitate his attendance? Please let me know as soon as possible. Love. Aunt Jim in Jamaica.

Looks like I'll be heading to the concrete jungle in June!

Note 25: Rats in the Kitchen! (email to my friends)

Oh! I've got to tell you about this! So I'm sitting in my apartment the other day, and I hear some banging that seems to be coming from just outside the kitchen. I stop to listen, and the banging stops. I resume what I'm doing on the laptop and the banging starts again. I look over to the kitchen and I see a rabbit on the sink. Well, I THOUGHT it was a rabbit. I mean it was as BIG as a rabbit. Fact is it was a freakin' RAT!!! Man, that sucker was so big, and I could see into its eyes so clearly that I could see its soul! We locked eyes for a second and then he (or she) bolted out the open kitchen window into the night.

The next day I asked the super to get one of the mesh screens for that window. It had been the only window in the apartment that didn't have a screen. So I went to bed the next night safe in the knowledge that this humongous trash-dweller, along with the mosquitoes that had been plaguing me at nights would be kept out.

Well, my friends, this was no ordinary rat! This was a rodent on a mission. I woke to find the screen mesh eaten through, one mango nibbled, and another mango missing off the kitchen counter!! Understand now that most rats that I'm used to—the ones from THIS planet—don't lift up 1/4lb mangoes and carry them off a plate of fruit, across a stove, and up a window sill, through a mesh screen and into the night! I was dealing with a different sort of rodent here.

The next day, after showing the super what happened, he laughed for a while, and then brought me a heavier gage mesh screen and installed it. But I was taking no chances this time. The next night I kept the glass window locked even though the mesh was there, just to see what would happen. Sure enough, the next morning I woke to find this:

The ENTIRE bottom half of the mesh had been ripped out! I could see smudges on the glass from where this rabid rat was banging, probably wondering to itself what the &$)%($&% I thought I was doing interfering with his nightly routine!

So now I keep the kitchen window permanently closed, and keep a watchful eye on other signs of forced entry around the apartment. I wouldn't put past this criminal-minded rodent the potential for gnawing through plaster, or just letting himself in through the front door! I'm not even going to TRY setting a trap. He'd probably pick it up, carry it up to my bedroom and snap it on my freakin' nose while I slept just to make a point! Damn!

My friend Adrienne replies:

Walt, I'm in stitches and horrified at the same time about the RAT!!! I would have left him the mangos, window screens, and the entire apt. I don't know if I'd survive. I'm a true city gal - or at least I think I am....LOL!

Adrienne,

I'm laughing about you leaving the rat with the mangos, the mesh and the apartment! But now that I think about it, it's probably HIS apartment! After all, I'm the visitor here. The apartment was "empty" when I got here, so he was here long before me, and, that means, oh, my gosh, *I'M* the intruder!!!

He's probably sitting outside with his head in his little paws, plotting how to get this big human out of his &$(%$(% apartment!!!! *I can only imagine the story he's telling HIS friends, or perhaps his wife:...*

"I tell you, Gertrude, he was HUGE!!"

Gertrude: "What do you mean we lost the apartment????"
Harvey: "I tell you Gertrude, I don't know what happened! I'm coming through the kitchen window like I ALWAYS do, right? I walk across the counter like I ALWAYS do, right? But THIS time, no, this time something is different, I can feel it. First of all, there were these mangoes on the counter...I swear I didn't put them there, but hey, with my rat's 30-second attention span, who can be sure..."

"Anyhoo, I get to the kitchen sink, and WHOAAA, there it was!!! I tell you I've never seen anything like it! This was no ordinary human! He was looking at me...man his eyes were so big I could see into his soul!! I tell ya, I high tailed it outta there!"

"Next day the kitchen window is blocked, but I got through, whew! But the next day, the glass was there!"
Gertrude: "Well you march right back there and do what we rats do, Harvey! Leave droppings, move things around, get all the fellows together and just pester the heck outta him. Gnaw everything in sight! I mean that's how we ran those first intruders out and got the apartment in the first place, isn't it??"
Harvey: "Yes, honey, but the glass, I can't cut through the glass!!"
Gertrude: "Did I marry a mouse or a gerbil, Harvey???"
    THE SAGA OF HARVEY THE RAT CONTINUES IN AN UPCOMING EPISODE OF THE SAIPAN CHRONICLES....
    Anyway, on to sweeter matters....

Note 26: Dating, Language and Culture

First Date, Thai Style

So I went to hang out with some Thai girls last night. A young lady I'll call "M" invited me to accompany her on what I figured was their girls' night out. We meet at Godfather's Bar in Garapan. They're all speaking Thai the entire night...but I didn't feel out of place. I guess it's a common thing in a place like Saipan, and especially on dates. I felt like I was part of the conversation even though our direct "in English" interaction was minimal. They were talking *about* me, talking *for* me, talking *to* me, asking M about me, so I was pretty involved in the evening although I couldn't speak a word of Thai to save my life.

M is actually leaving Saipan later today to go back to Thailand. She did teach me a few words I can use when I visit her.

Hmmm...Now that I think about it, someone told me that especially among Thai girls, according to the *Thai Book of Rules for Dating*, it's not unusual for a first date to have a gang of chaperones—brother, sister, friends, even mother and father—along for the date. And now that I think of it, M *was* the only one dressed up in a skirt and heels like she was on a date, while the others were casually dressed. And she had no problem holding my hand when we were walking even with all her friends around. So, this was probably NOT the girls' night out that I thought it was....oh, my goodness, this was a first date!!

First Date, Chinese-style

So I met this nice young lady (I'll call her A) in a supermarket. We went out last week. As I mentioned, first dates on this side of the world can often be group events. Anyway, A, only brought along one person: her friend B. So picture the three of us, me walking side by side with A and B who are walking with their arms locked together—best friend style. Ain't it great! Anyway, she and I went out again last night (no friend this time, so guess I passed the test!) I've had to revise some of my rules and requirements when it comes to dating. If I asked a woman out while living in New York, and she said "can I bring my friend along?" it would be a sure sign that she was not interested. Here, I've discovered it actually may mean the exact opposite.

Communication

Dating across cultural and language barriers is a pretty interesting adventure. I'm finding myself to be a different person when it comes to relationships.

Not having the "advantage" of language forces me to keep things really simple. I've been told I can be a master at evasion and subtlety. But one can only beat around the bush when one has an extensive vocabulary the subtleties of which *both* people can understand. Bushes for beating around and hiding behind become sparse when the words aren't there. So, if X from China is still learning English, and I only speak Chinese in short "small talk" type sentences, then when we *do* communicate, it has to be more direct, less flowery, and our needs and desires are kept very basic.

This level of communication also forces me to give up and release stuff that I might otherwise hammer to death, rehash in seven different ways 'til Sunday, exploring all the permutations, combinations and ramifications, and all the *"what did you mean when you said this"* stuff that people often get into when they have fights. I just let it go. In other words, if you have a disagreement or misunderstanding with your significant other, you (have to) get to the 'forgive and move on' stage rather quickly, since the disagreement or misunderstanding might have been caused by the communication disadvantage, and, you can't really argue about it for hours on end, for the same reason.

While communication is a critical part of relationship, I find that a person's spirit and energy and even sense of humor transcend the limits of language. The things that attract one person to another are first and foremost always of a non-verbal nature. I've had communication, albeit of a perfunctory and superficial nature with Japanese, Koreans, etc., with neither of us speaking each others' language quite that well. There are some universal gestures, body language, and the ever-reliable smile that can go a long way.

In the interest of following one's attractions, one finds ways of coping with this "barrier" of language. "I'm a man. You're a woman. I like you. You like me." Life can be pretty simple.

I've been to clubs, festivals, parties, weddings and all sorts of gatherings and have been meeting some very nice people. But, unless you're in my "close friends" loop, you probably won't get to see those *Jamaican on Saipan* adventures. Sorry!

Now, just as I'm settling in, just as I found a stash of cookies for my sweet tooth, and started my dating life, as you'll recall, NY calls!

Note 27: Return to New York: Unnecessary Roughness

I head to NY to pick up my dad for us to travel together for a family reunion in Canada. I wrote the following for my weekly *Saipan Tribune* article while in NY:

Originally published July 26, 2006
First of all, I should state for the record that I'm not a politician, an economist or an urban planner. I'm an entrepreneur with a penchant for marketing. Having said that, let me say that I'm now in New York City. I had a family gathering to attend a few weeks ago and have extended my stay just a bit longer.

As I landed in New York, one of the first things I noticed as I waited in line to pass through customs and immigration was the amount and level of coughing, sneezing and throat clearing among the crowd...seems people are a bit sicker, or at least more 'congested' here. Next, as I boarded a bus to take me home from the airport, my bag hit the leg of a young lady sitting in the front seat. Her response was to level a volley of a few choice curses in my general direction...seems people are bit angrier, and less forgiving here, too. Later that week, as I drove up the Henry Hudson Parkway on Manhattan's west side, I noticed, to my chagrin, that the water alternated between an odd shade of brown and gray...seems things are a bit more polluted here, as well. Throughout my stay, as I dealt with cashiers, and subway token booth clerks, and waiters and waitresses, I encountered a distinct and noticeable level of hostility, impatience and general "service with bad attitude" throughout. (I thought to myself that it was a far cry from the effusive 3-part harmony "good morning, sir!" that I receive from the young ladies at the front registers at Dolphin Wholesale.)

Yes, it seems there's a level of stress, tension, anger, unhappiness, anxiety and hostility that pervades virtually every facet of life and human interaction here. Now don't get me wrong, I don't want you to think I'm bashing New York. Having lived here for most of my life, I realize it has much going for it—as a mecca of opportunity, a world center of finance, fashion, shopping, culture and cuisine—nothing compares to the Big Apple. But it got me thinking: Why so hostile?

Years ago, I had a long conversation with my uncle and cousin about why it was that when we all lived in Jamaica, we saw more of each other than when we lived in New York, even though we lived comparatively closer geographically when in NY. I'll spare you the ins and outs of the conversation and cut to the chase: We concluded the reason was that there was more access to nature's abundance in Jamaica. Mango trees lined the streets. Star apples, breadfruit, sweetsop trees could be found along any highway. Everyone had some sort of fruit tree in his/her back yard.

Now, you may naturally ask, why is that important, and what does it have do with the frequency of interaction within a family living abroad? Well, we reasoned it this way: as a result of this relatively easy access to nature, life and sustenance, there is a tendency for people to share that abundance. Living in Jamaica, it's not uncommon for a neighbor to gift you with bags of mangos, oranges, cherries or whatever happens to be in season. If they don't, it'll simply fall from the trees, rot and go to waste. We lose nothing by sharing nature's bounty (it's the same on Saipan). In contrast, that simple freedom is one that very few New Yorkers have.

Sure, people can be kind-hearted and give of anything they wish wherever they reside. But the difference in a city like New York is that any and everything you own, you had to purchase it. The tradeoff of living in the land of opportunity stacked one atop another in fifty-floor apartment buildings is that there are no backyards with mango trees, no landscapes with guava trees and coconuts. In New York, a dozen mangos would cost you about $17. If you earn the minimum wage of about $7 per hour, that's 2+ hours of work you've had to exchange for those mangos. Two hours of your life. Two hours of freedom. Therefore, it does not go unnoticed on a subconscious level that, since there are no backyard mango trees to replace them, that to give them away is to give away something very valuable. There is a tendency, therefore, faced with such a sense of scarcity, to accumulate, hoard and prize those things of value that one has had to work so hard for. This tendency to hoard extends to the thing of most value that the average person trades for money in a capitalistic society: their time.

So when the weekend comes, or in truth *any* opportunity for rest from the daily grind, one is more likely to value one's rest and relaxation time and, since it's so easy to do so—with television, cable, home delivery of videos and pizza—insulate and isolate oneself from the outside world. Hence little time for spending with others. (And Jamaicans, stereotypically known as hard workers with multiple jobs, like many immigrants in search of the American dream, perhaps make themselves busier and scarcer than most).

Yes, in the industrialized society everything comes at a price. Food comes at a price. Nature comes at a price. Beauty comes at a price. People pay thousands each year to vacation in far away lands, and essentially have to pay for access to the food, natural beauty, white sands and blue oceans we have in abundance in Jamaica, and here on Saipan. Which brings me, finally, to my point.

As we here in the CNMI strive to compete, survive and thrive in the global industrialized marketplace, it is vitally important that those in key positions of power and decision-making realize just what is at stake. It is important that in the pursuit of profit, paradise does not fall victim. (But more on that later)

Note 28: Jamaican in Canada

As I mentioned, I was in Canada for my Aunt's 80th birthday celebration and family reunion. Throughout the day (which was also Canada Day), family and friends from all over Canada and the states stopped by her farm in Ottawa to wish her well!

The former mayor presented her with a plaque in gratitude for her activism and contributions

Note 29: Preserving Paradise

As promised, I'll continue the thoughts I started in Note 27. If you remember what Jamaica was like in the 1970s, then you might remember when you could drive from Spanish Town to Old Harbour, during the middle of the day, and a car would pass you going the opposite direction. You could wait a full minute before another would pass. That's how traffic is on some main streets here on Saipan.

If you remember what Jamaica was like in the 1960s, then you might remember a time when you could sleep with your front door open, and wake the next day and still find all your possessions right where you left them. That's what life is like on Saipan.

Sure there's crime here, but one thing that stood out during my first month here was a report on the 6 o'clock television news about a tourist's laptop being stolen. Petty thefts like that generally don't make headlines in New York. The fact it did is an indication of the size of the island, but also its stage of 'development.' It's that kind of lifestyle, that kind of humanity, the kind of community that exists before 'foreign' ways intrude and alter the internal and external landscape that I feel strongly about preserving.

I have the perspective of being from a land where I've seen the effects of what tourism can do to an island. I've seen what an unbridled focus on emulating the best and worst of industrialized nations can do to an island's people. It's with that in mind that I wrote and published the following piece for the *Saipan Tribune*:

Note 30: The 10 Commandments of Paradise
by Walt Goodridge-published Saipan Tribune *Aug 2, 2006*

[Begin article]

As I stated last week, the development and economic resuscitation that we pursue must not perpetuate the cycle of decay. We must not lose our unique value in a misguided notion of what constitutes progress. We must never become so blinded by wealth that we miss the long-term effects of what we are doing to achieve it.

Ever since coming to Saipan and falling in love with its natural beauty, I've been working on some concepts to help everyone, not just those in power, maintain what we may often take for granted. I call them The 10 Commandments of Paradise:

The 10 Commandments of Paradise

PREAMBLE: In the pursuit of progress, we must find solutions that ensure our survival, sustain our environment, honor our traditions, conserve our resources, respect our culture and preserve the right and ability of every generation to enjoy life in a natural environment in the same or better condition as that of the previous generation. Therefore,

1. We shall not allow industrialization to assume more importance than the individual, nor, in the pursuit of profit neglect what is in the best long-term interests of our own nation and its inhabitants.

2. We shall not let the unchecked depletion of natural resources nor the manipulation of the natural environment destroy our access to, nor our enjoyment of the pristine beauty of our land, sea and air.

3. We shall not allow another nation's political agenda to subvert our allegiance to truth and justice, nor influence us to make decisions not in our best interests.

4. We shall not allow another nation's interpretation of history to distort our own perspective, nor limit our right to advance our own.

5. We shall not allow another society's language, religion or education to overshadow our own.

6. We shall not allow misguided ideas of health and medicine to undermine time-honored traditions, nor our reliance on proven, natural methods of healing.

7. We shall not allow another society's concepts of entertainment, fashion, beauty, food or lifestyle to replace our respect and reverence for the fruits of our own culture.

8. We shall not allow another individual's or nation's concepts of morality to distort our own.

9. We shall not allow another individual's or nation's choices to influence our own sense of ethics.

10. And, in the pursuit of solutions to the challenges we will surely face in implementing all of the above, we shall endeavor to offer the world a new paradigm of progress, one that protects while it profits, one that elevates while not excluding, expands without exploiting, so that we can preserve paradise in the way we found it.

So, yes, you can call me an idealist. I'll wear the badge with pride. But I also believe that at the heart of idealism must be ideas. So I'd like to be part of those offering ideas for progress that don't perpetuate the negative aspects of capitalism. See, the trouble with capitalism is that it has traditionally been based on the depletion model, without regard to, or simply oblivious to the effects of the thrust for more and cheaper. As a result, our global society now experiences the effects of over-farming, overproduction, over-foresting, etc. on land, sea and air in the form of global warming, depleted soil, lowered air quality, rampant livestock disease and a host of other ills.

Saipan, its leadership, and the new wave of Saipanpreneurs, in developing plans for the region, the economy, as well as the working and living conditions of its citizens, must develop ideas that preserve as well as profit; export without exhausting; selling without selling out.

And again, while I don't have the daunting task of leading a nation, creating economic models, or planning a society, I do know that in the implementation of any ideal, where there is a will, there is a way!

I believe that the old way is on its way out. I predict there will be a shift and a crumbling of industries and thought forms based on the depletion and exploitation models of progress. It's already happening in many areas. The people are ready for it. Indeed the world, as an entity, is starved for it. The old models will be replaced with models of sustainability, eco-friendliness, emission-reduction, etc. The CNMI can be one of the regions that shows the world the way.

So the questions we ask must change. Do we have anything other than cheap labor and tax incentives to offer investors? How can we preserve the balance and beauty of our islands even as we offer access to increasing numbers of tourists? How can we replace and improve even as we mine and export? How can we, as doctors are supposed to, practice our craft and reach our goals while doing no harm? How can we profit and leave things even better than how we found it? These questions have answers. The answers can be found by those brave enough to ask the questions and seek the optimal solutions outside of traditional ways of thinking.

Here's an example of something called CARBON TRADING, from an article I read online by David Oglaza, the founder of GuideMeGreen.com

The basic premise of carbon trading is this: Firms are set quotas on how much carbon dioxide they can produce per year, if they produce more than this allowance, then they must buy an allowance from another firm that has not reached its quota on how much it can produce in one year! The idea of the carbon-trading scheme was to raise the cost to firms of continuing to pollute while creating a market to give an incentive to become more environmentally efficient. Units of these quotas are traded in a similar way to buying and selling shares. The potential benefits of such a system for developing countries would be that poorer, developing countries can "sell" their "surplus" carbon dioxide quotas to richer countries. This income could stimulate much needed economic growth. They could also achieve their Kyoto commitments at the lowest possible cost as the money needed to invest in cleaner technology can be funded by the trading on carbon units." For more details visit www.guidemegreen.com.

Finding answers like this is imperative, for if they are not found and implemented, Saipan may find itself richer in one sense, but with brown waters, dimmer skies, manicured landscapes and with a surly population coughing and sneezing as they snarl their unhappiness at unsuspecting tourists and citizens alike. We would lose the very things that make this paradise. And that, my friend, would make us woefully poorer in the long run.

[End of article]

Note 31: Paradise-preneurs

Originally appeared in the Saipan Tribune on April 25, 2007

Someone asked me recently what sort of business I would start here on Saipan. To lay the foundation for my response, I'd like to introduce you to a term with which you're probably already familiar. The term is "catalyst."

As you may remember from high school chemistry class, a catalyst is a substance that ignites, sets in motion, or speeds up a reaction without itself being affected. In life as well, every experience is a potential catalyst. Your flat tire, the argument with your spouse, your unhappiness at your job—all are potential catalysts. Because of the free will inherent in our experience here on the planet (we have the freedom to choose our responses), the reaction that a catalyst can spark is entirely under your control.

THE PURPOSE OF CATALYSTS

All catalysts are designed to offer a challenge or lesson. There are only two possible paths one can choose in response to a catalyst: It can be accepted or it can be controlled. The path you choose will be determined by your orientation. If you are oriented towards service to <u>self</u> (i.e. your own comfort), you will make one set of choices. If you are oriented towards service to <u>others</u>, you will see and choose from a different set of choices.

When faced with a catalyst, it is important to understand that we are all here to evolve in the direction of our orientation, and without life's catalysts, the desire to evolve and the faith in the process do not normally manifest, and thus evolution does not occur. Therefore, don't rail against life's challenges. Accept them as a natural part of the experience designed to help you evolve.

Life is simple: Things happen. Choose your response based on your orientation. Evolve in the direction of your choice.

But you *must* choose. When neither path is chosen, the catalyst fails in its design, and you proceed through life until some other catalyst appears which causes you to choose again towards acceptance and love or toward separation and control.

HOW TO PREDICT THE FUTURE

It's a basic law of this dynamic, ever-changing universe that there's no such thing as something "staying the same." Things are either expanding or contracting, increasing or decreasing, getting better or getting worse. Even the metal or hard plastic computer or sheet of paper on which you are reading these words, as solid and as stable as they seem are all slowly decaying and deteriorating. Come back in a few dozen years, and you'll see the effects of decay over time. If you know this, then you can look at everything from business phenomena to romantic relationships a little bit differently, and can perform what some might consider fortune-telling simply by asking, "where is this heading?"

Every business, every situation, every relationship is either getting better or getting worse, growing or shrinking, going up or heading downhill. Therefore, as long as you can honestly assess what you observe or experience over a given time frame, you can "predict" where something is heading and take any evasive or remedial actions as necessary.

Now having said that, let's examine some observable facts and trends in catalysts occurring right now and that will affect the future, and to which we have a choice of response.

1. The earth is going through changes.

Global warming is a reality. Temperature fluctuations are affecting access to water, arable land and other resources for a growing segment of the world's population. These and other physical, climatic, and cataclysmic changes are observable.

2. "Peak Oil" is a reality.

The term "peak oil" refers to the peak in the world's oil production. The amount of oil available on the planet is finite. There is a point in oil production whether within a single oil field or the entire planet, when a maximum is reached. Once that maximum rate of production is reached, the rate of oil production (and the profitability of extracting it) enters a terminal decline. The challenge this presents is that while the SUPPLY is declining, the DEMAND for oil (i.e. oil-dependent plastics, electricity, etc.) continues to increase as population and industrialization grow. It's said that US oil production peaked in 1970. World oil production, it is said by some, peaked in 2005. After a peak, production slows, profits decrease, and prices rise. You can already see the effects of this as gas prices creep upwards.

3. Corporate downsizing persists

More and more companies are outsourcing, downsizing and offshoring in an effort to cut costs. Companies, particularly public corporations, are bound by their charters and by law to seek first the profitability of their shareholders. That's why the decisions these companies make often seem less humanitarian and more profit-inspired. That's because they have to be.

4. Global power and focus is shifting

China and India are growing economic forces. They represent sources of labor, consumers, as well as increased oil and energy demand. Companies the world over in Europe, and the US, are importing laborers from China, or outsourcing skilled jobs to India.

DON'T SLEEP

As a potential entrepreneur, indeed as a nation, the opportunity exists to predict, anticipate, prepare for and position oneself for the effects of these trends. Don't wait for mainstream news broadcasts to confirm this. Don't expect politicians to make it part of their agendas in time. They are operating from a different agenda. Those who seek to rule the world are by nature unlike those of the world they seek to rule.

THE CHALLENGE

As I said, there is always either a lesson or a challenge.

Within the context of these trends, the CNMI's economic condition, and by extension, your unique situation is a catalyst that provides an opportunity for you to respond in search of a lesson or a challenge. As potential entrepreneurs, if we choose to rise to the challenge, using what we know about predicting the future, the question becomes first: *What's going to happen as these trends and catalysts continue?* And then more importantly, *what shall I do in response to these happenings?* Where should I look for the opportunity? What sort of business would I start? And finally which business path offers the most opportunity for service to others?

Now there are those who would ask, 'which path offers the most profit?' That's a *service-to-self* orientation. We need a new paradigm. I suggest, as motivational speaker Zig Ziglar is credited with saying, that if you help enough people get what *they* want, you automatically get what *you* want.

(As an aside, in your personal life, when faced with a catalyst, as you search for the lesson, ask yourself which path offers the lesson of patience, tolerance and the ability for the light touch?)

MY THOUGHTS ON THE COMING SHIFT

There's another important trend that I believe is important to factor into this equation, and it is this: *The continued growth upon which the current economic model is based cannot be sustained indefinitely.* Infinite growth based on finite resources is unsustainable. Growth based on the exploitation of others is unethical, untenable, and also unsustainable.

Yes, China and India are both ideal sources of labor as well as the next great frontier for consumerism. The rest of the world's industrialized, market-driven, capitalist, consumer-oriented companies and entrepreneurs know this as well, and are rushing to position themselves.

However, the gold watch-sporting, cola-drinking, junk food-eating, luxury car-driving, soap opera-watching, video game-playing lifestyle upon which these companies rely to support their spiritually vapid, environmentally-depleting and mindless products, while exploiting the poor as the labor source, is on an inevitable decline. Global consciousness of a more serious nature is actually on the rise (it's just not being reported).

So if you see, as I do, the potential crash of the entire economic system upon which this model hinges, then you might agree that basing a new industry or business idea on such shifting sand, while perpetuating a soon-to-be outdated business model that separates and destroys the family structure, enslaves communities, while perpetuating indentured servitude is not a desirable course.

So, here is the challenge in a nutshell. The current model is unsustainable. We need to survive. However, our survival is based on buying into a definition of success that perpetuates the very model threatening our survival. What then, should be our best course of action?

THE ETHICAL PARADOX OF SELLING SURVIVAL

How do you survive in an economic system that is threatening your and its own survival? Answer: You sell survival. That's right, the game is changing to one of selling survival.

Right now others in the know are mobilizing to prepare to offer you their solutions. But what they offer won't be real solutions. They will offer products, services and a paradigm which perpetuates their control and their *individual* survival. In some parts of the world, companies are already charging the population for access to clean water, and some are selling seeds which have been genetically altered to produce single-generation crops forcing farmers into a cycle of having to purchase new seeds every season just to survive.

But how do you survive in good conscience by profiting from what others need to survive? Therein lies the paradox of selling survival. But that sort of response is not the option. Selling altered seeds or clean water is not the survival I wish to sell. If I were starting a business, I would follow the experts who predict that the stated trends will favor business models that:

1. anticipate coming global shifts in social interaction and lifestyles (i.e. tribal living in larger social families that are self-supporting; ones that engage in more efficient means of creating energy, obtaining food, and supporting the common welfare)

2. offer people the means of survival given the "peak oil" phenomenon (i.e. alternative fuel sources, power generation capacities, solar, wind, insulating technologies)

3. utilize technology in ways that empower and free the exploited from the manual labor which keeps them at the lower rungs of the totem pole

Wouldn't it be nice to jump ahead of the curve and start or join an industry, or launch a new business that helps the most people, prepares for coming earth changes, empowers rather than exploits the labor pool, reduces dependence on diminishing energy resources, offers the consumer real alternatives, while at the same time offers the world a new paradigm and consciousness as it relates to survivability, sustainability, adding our voice and actions to the very change in consciousness and alternate paradigm that our very survival necessitates? Yep, that would be pretty cool. And that's what *I* would do from here in Paradise.

...*at the end of every rainbow in paradise...There's a low-hanging, double-rainbow in this shot you may not be able to see in the black & white paperback edition of this book.*

These are my thoughts—as a Jamaican—on Saipan. These are my thoughts—as an entrepreneur—on business, ethics and moving forward not just on Saipan, but in a world facing numerous global challenges. I've compiled more of these essays and articles into a manifesto entitled "The New Saipan" which you may find free of charge at www.newsaipan.com.

Note 32: My World

My world is free of judgment
I see all men as themselves
No biases, no prejudice,
no boxes and no shelves

My world's based on the premise
that innately man is good
Wayward at times but given choice
treats others as he should

My world's not complicated
For the heart's bliss is the goal
A world free of deception
where no one seeks control

My world's based on abundance
and no one need live in lack
No good can come through building wealth
upon on another's back

My world's free of pollution
we respect land, air and seas
As stewards are we charged
and on this everyone agrees

My world's a fun adventure
one where innocence survives
The spark of youthful wonderment
persists for all our lives

My world is here to give you hope
and share with you this news
Your life can be your dream
So dream the world that you would choose

As a business coach, and the author of books designed to help people live more passion-centered lives, I couldn't write this book without some aspect of my mission coming to the fore. With that said, however, we shall now return to the regular scheduled *Jamaican On Saipan* adventure still in progress!

Note 33: Breaking News! WALT'S FRIDAY INSPIRATION EMAIL ENDS NINE YEAR RUN

August 18, 2006

On August 18, 2006, while back in New York after attending my aunt's 80th birthday celebration, I officially ended my 9-year run doing the *Walt's Friday Inspiration* email! I received a lot of emails of congratulations and also inquiries into what's next.

Here is the email I sent out in response:

Dear Subscriber,

Last week's 468th weekly Friday Inspiration life Rhyme marked exactly 9 years of consecutive intentional communication with you my readers. As nine is a number of completion, and since 468 straight weeks, while just a blip on the radar screen of eternity, is a good chunk of time on this earth plane, I've decided to bring to a close this chapter of my journey. Therefore, last week's edition was the final in the Walt's Friday Inspiration emails. (Sorry for the short notice!)

Yes, on August 29, 1997 I sent the first Friday Inspiration email to a small group of friends and business partners. It featured a simple quote I had written years earlier for my college yearbook:

> *"The road to the top*
> *is for those who gamble*
> *with life's uncertainties,*
> *and who view setbacks*
> *as opportunities to excel!"*

--Walt Goodridge, (College Yearbook)
President, a company called W

Ending this nine-year run, this weekly tradition, this line of communication with you is a bit scary. It's been part of a formula I've used to create the freedom and impact I now experience. It's been a constant for myself and my readers that we all have looked forward to. I've enjoyed the tremendous feedback over the years and of learning how the life rhymes have impacted so many lives. Yes, ending them opens things up to a degree of uncertainty. But it's an uncertainty I'm eager to gamble with.

I've been greatly inspired these past few days by two books entitled (1) *Bringers of the Dawn*, and (2) *Earth: Pleiadian Keys to the Living Library*, both by Barbara Marciniak. Within the pages of those books, I've found an echoing of who I am and much of what I've endeavored to accomplish throughout my life. This quote in particular resonated with me:

"It is time for you to make a commitment to create joy, creativity and love for yourself. Only then will you benefit others, for if you do not evolve yourself, you do not serve others. By becoming a living example, by following what is in your heart, you show the way for others to follow with courage what is in their hearts."

It's another way of expressing what has always been my mantra and mission from day one:

*"I share what I know,
so that others may grow"*

I've come to realize beyond doubt that my life is a story to be told; that part of why I am here is to be that living example. So, even this act of embracing change and uncertainty is just another chapter in an ongoing story.

For those of you who have followed the story for these many years, I sincerely thank you for joining me on this journey. But, don't worry, I'm still here. The journey does not yet end. It merely shifts gears, turns corners, takes detours and evolves.

I'm excited by this change, even though I have no full or concrete idea of what I shall choose to become next. What I do know is that I intend to continue to be part of the revolution of thought and evolution of practice that will inspire, ignite and issue change among those of us who are here.

For those of you who have followed along for these many years, I sincerely thank you for joining me on this journey. I hope you'll join me for Chapter Next.

Walt F.J. Goodridge
The Passion Prophet
www.passionprofit.com
Catch all the prior episodes by visiting www.liferhymes.com,

Time to head back to Saipan!

Note 34: Escape from America...The Sequel! This time it's personal.....and embarrassing!

Thursday, Sept 14, 2006

I'm in New York again. What would another escape from America be without a little departure drama story to tell?

Well, I'm sitting here on flight 333 to Houston. But once again, I almost didn't make it! No, I didn't need a visa this time. All my tickets were paid for. No this would turn out to be a different drama. But I'll get to it all in a second. Let me start from the beginning.

At 5:00 a.m. on Thursday September 14, I stepped out of my apartment with three bulging bags of undetermined weights. (I wasn't able to procure a scale to weigh them in advance.) As I stood in the dark morning drizzle on Lennox Avenue and 119th Street, a taxi honked to get my attention and I indicated my assent to ride. So far so good, but I first had to convince the driver to take me to LaGuardia for all of the $28 I had in my wallet at the time. As he explained to me, with $9 in tolls to and back, he would net only $19 for the trip.... way below the going rate.

As we stood in the rain with him contemplating the feasibility of the fare, I shoved the money in his hands, showed him my empty wallet and waited for him to decide. (I've always found that "cash in hand" is a great persuasion tool. Since rush hour traffic was just beginning, we make it to the airport in good time. I thank him. He wishes me good luck, and I hobble inside.

Once at the ticket counter, my bags are weighed and they're each coming in dangerously close to the 50-lb limit. One bag was 53.5 lbs, another was 48.5lbs and another was 33.5. So I was told I'd have to move things around to reduce the heavier one. So there I am with my garment bag spread out on the floor in front of the ticket agent while searching for 3.5lbs of items to move around.

As I find various objects to move, the ticket agent says, "Mr. Goodridge? Do you have a receipt for your return from Saipan? You have to show a return ticket, or you can't go."

I freeze like a deer in headlights, as I ponder at lightning speed what the heck I'm going to do now.

"Well, I thought that was a two way ticket," I said weakly.

"Well, I'm not showing a return booking. When did you book to return?" she asks.

"October 29th?" I lied.

"I'm not showing you booked on any flights. You either have to show a receipt....Or you can book one now," she suggests.

Book one now, I think to myself. *That's easy for you to say. I just gave my last $28 to a taxi driver who's on his way back to Harlem."*

"How much does a flight cost?" I ask.

"When do you want to fly?" she asks.

Who gives a crap!!!?? Just find a &$(*%$(% flight! I wanted to scream. I opted instead to say: "Anytime, I'm flexible. Make it for Oct 29." I suggest.

"What time do you want to leave Saipan?" she inquires further.

Look, lady, you're trying me! I want to reply, but again opt instead for: "There's a morning flight every day out of Saipan if I'm not mistaken."

She finds a flight from Saipan to Guam for $91. Whew! That's a relief. I was fully expecting a $600 plus fare to add some more intense drama to this story. But it didn't really matter either way as I still had no space available on my credit card (yes, even Passion Prophets have occasional cash flow "situations.") So, I handed her my credit card nonchalantly (knowing fully well it would probably be declined.

"Do you have another card?" she asks after a brief pause. "This one was declined."

I nonchalantly hand her my other card. (Wonder how long I can play this game until a better strategy comes to me?)

"Sorry, sir, this one is declined also."

"I'll need to see a receipt for an outgoing flight."

"I'll book it online," I said.

"Well, we don't have a computer you can use," she says. "And we don't have internet access."

What is she in the dark ages??

"I have a laptop," I explain, "and the concourse is wired."

"Ok, but you only have 20 minutes to make the booking."

Twenty minutes!? Is she kidding me? Doesn't she know I've designed websites launched them online and started getting customers in less time? Twenty minutes is a friggin' lifetime! Booking a ticket online should be a piece of cake. All I need is um...a valid credit card. So, I'll have to call my friends.

Yep, that's right, it's 5:45 a.m., as in morning, and I'm going to call my friends to beg for money! (This would be embarrassing, if I really cared.)

I call my friends A. and S., a married couple with two kids. No answer. Voicemail. Drat! Sleeping, perhaps? (You think??)

I call my buddy E. He'll be awake. But as the call starts to connect, my phone goes dead....battery charge ran out. I ask a ticket agent if there's an electrical outlet I can use to plug in and she directs me to one a few feet from the ticket counters. So I leave my bags open on the floor, with stuff strewn about and go sit on the floor next to the outlet. I plug in my phone and wait a bit for the charge to take. E, a motorman for the MTA, is actually in the middle of this shift. Yes, he's driving a #3 train somewhere in Brooklyn. I get through to him, and through a barely audible, touch and go cell phone connection, I tell him I need his credit card. He tells me he's one station away from going underground at the Utica Ave station. *FYI: Once underground it'll be at least another hour before he's above ground again and able to receive any calls.* His signal starts breaking up, as he starts reading the credit card number to me, (tick, tock) I can hear the conductor in the background saying "Watch the closing doors," signaling E. to start the train and get moving to the next station.

Having ridden in the motorman's cab with him before, I can picture him steering the train with one hand, going a bit slower than usual to keep from losing our connection, while reading the credit card numbers in the darkness of the cabin. (tick, tock, tick tock)

I repeat the numbers back to him, ring off, (or perhaps we were cut off) and then I use the card first to log into the paid wi-fi service available in the concourse. After two attempts, (sorry, E, I'll paypal you the $15.98) I get through. (Time is ticking away!) I log on to continental.com, find the same flight and price the agent had found from her terminal, and I book it as quickly as I can. (tick tock, tick tock!)

"Have you booked it yet, sir?" The agent calls out to me. "You only have about 5 minutes." It's now about 6:15am. Boarding for my flight is beginning about now.

Then, I get an error message!! The screen says the card number is not valid! Uh-oh. But I know it should be ok, so I check it again and realize that when I had copied it to paste it into the form, I had inadvertently included an extra blank space at the end of the numbers. I deleted the space, tried again, and.....and.....and...

.

...success!
"Your ticket purchase is confirmed!" That screen was music to my.... um, eyes???!! Anyway, I walk over to ticket counter, show the agent the confirmation number, she finds it in the system, but says it's not ticketed yet. I show her the confirmation screen on my laptop which shows the completed purchase. But she says she can't do anything until it's actually ticketed. No one knows just how long it takes for a just-purchased ticket to get ticketed, so we wait—me with baited breath, she probably thinking *when's my coffee break?*

In about a minute, she says, "Ok, you're good to go!"

I gather and continue packing my bags, having been laid out on the terminal floor with books and an external drive (about 3.5lbs) resting on one of the bags.

I rush to the security checkpoint, where I'm instructed to remove all metals from my pockets, remove my sandals, remove my laptop from its bag and place all objects on the conveyor belt. I then pass through the metal detector and wait on the other side.

As my carry-on goes through the x-ray machine, I hear an agent say to a coworker, "Pots?? What's the story with pots?" referring to my pressure cooker and stainless steel pots bulging the seams of my carry-on. His buddy comes to look. I'm sure neither of them knows whether this presents a hijack risk (I may whip out my utensils and start a food fight at 30,000 feet, you never know), but at that time of the morning, neither of them wanted the hassle to do the research. So everything's approved. I proceed to gate A-4, where boarding is already in process. I have a few minutes, so I head to the men's room, change from my sweatshirt and jeans and into my Guru Gear. (Have to look spiffy for my return to Paradise!) I board the plane, settle into seat 5-F and get ready for takeoff!

In the men's room donning guru-gear for the return to Saipan!

The rest of my trip proceeds without any drama.

PART 1: HOUSTON: Leg #1 of the journey (to Houston) complete.

PART 2: TOKYO : 3:05 p.m. local time Friday afternoon. I'm now in Tokyo's Narita airport for a 5-hour layover until my flight to Guam. It's 2:05 a.m. Friday morning for you guys back in New York. I've been up and traveling for about 22 hours so far, and only half way home!

PART 3: GUAM: They took my tea tree oil, and one bottle of grapefruit seed extract! "No liquids on the plane," he says.

PART 4: SAIPAN: Just landed at 3:00 a.m. local time Saturday morning! That's 1:00 p.m. Friday afternoon New York time! So after 31 hours of travel from door to door, I'm finally home! Whew!

My friend Ernest is getting married in November, so chances are I'll be back in NY again quite soon.

Note 35: A Nomad Ruminates on the Concept of Home

On Sep 18, 2006
Nicole writes: [after reading my escape story]
Wow, Walt. What an ordeal. So, I'm just curious. You ended with "I'm finally home." Does this mean you don't consider NY your home anymore, or even Jamaica? :-)
Glad you made it there. Thank goodness for friends. Let's hang when you return. You ARE returning, aren't you?
Have a Blessed and Prosperous Day,
Nicole

Nicole,
Yep, thank goodness for friends!
Home? Hmmmm....that's always been a tough one for me to be clear about.
"Home" used to be Jamaica, and perhaps it still is ultimately when all is said and done. I think I may have told you all of this before, but perhaps I need to re-say it, for my own clarity.

I've never considered NY or America my home. It was the most familiar place to hang my hat since that's where I've lived most of my life, but it was never home. I returned there from Maryland because I knew people there and it was easier to resume life in a familiar place. But, as I've recently realized, it was chosen FOR me. I never chose to come here from Jamaica. Nor did I choose Jamaica, for that matter. If one looks at things purely from this plane of existence, it was through history and the "accident" of birth that I ended up there, but I never consciously chose

Jamaica either. (Yes, I believe from a metaphysical and spiritual perspective, my soul chose the parents, time and location of my arrival on this plane, but you know what I mean!)

Saipan, therefore, is the first country I've lived in that was by my own free will and choice. In that regard it represents a whole different ballgame of happiness.

Having said that, I'm also open-minded and adventurous in regard to where I live. So, by no means does this move represent anything final either.

I'm at a place in life where I'm enjoying the residual benefits of a lot of work I put in for the past 10 years (yes, even when it seemed like all I did was sit around at the computer when we lived together for that month before you kicked me out, this is what I was building) :-)

"It" is still not complete, but I can continue to build it at any pace and in any place that suits me, and so the goal is to simply experience more places.

I met a fellow here who is a merchant marine. He's been all around the world, and at my request, he gave me his top picks for places EVERY MAN NEEDS TO VISIT at least once:
1. Moorea, F Polynesia
2. Chile
3. Malta (St Julians)
4. Croatia (Zagreb)
5. China (Suzhou)
6. Taiwan (Kao Chung)
7. Sout Spain (Malaga)
8. Romania (Costanza)
9. Hungary (Siofok)

Mas, Clem and me. Thanks for the travel tips, Clem!

I'll be traveling to these places and enjoying life, and who knows, I may change into a completely different person along the way at any time.

So who knows? Perhaps there's no real home for a nomad, just a series of happy experiences on a never-ending journey.

I love you and all my friends I made while in America, and there is no way to minimize the tremendous impact you all, ACN, Columbia, the Port Authority, Tag Team and "The Briarwood 7" have had on my life. But it would not be beyond the realm of possibility that I simply sail off into the sunset and me, and all this becomes a pleasant memory of happy times gone by.

Yes, there is a sadness about it all as well. Separation brings with it a sense of loss and sorrow, I admit. But so too does happiness.

I want to be happy, and for now at least, happiness means honoring the call from afar, indulging my preferences, and never allowing myself to be bound by the familiar, or shackled by the chains of habit and circumstance. I can't allow NY to keep me simply because it has become habitual, no matter how sweet my friendships there are.

So, to answer your question, *"You ARE returning, aren't you?"* If you mean am I returning to New York for Ernest's wedding, the answer is yes. But if you mean shall I return to resume living in New York, then the answer is *"perhaps not."* There's no plan to. And just as I made and kept a promise to myself never to return to the corporate world, THIS move as well is based on the same kind of promise never to live somewhere that makes me unhappy.

Note 36: Saipan Food Co-op

Sept 30, 2006

While living in New York, I was a card-carrying member of the Park Slope Food Cooperative in Brooklyn. By definition, *A co-op is a member-owned, member-controlled business that operates for the mutual benefit of all members and according to common principles established for cooperatives*. Our food co-op provided primarily organic, locally-grown, low cost food and household items. The overriding principle was that of supporting companies and products which reduced negative environmental impact, improved sustainability, and offered healthy alternatives. Once I got back from New York, I recommitted myself to setting up something similar on Saipan. So, I set up a website, created a mission statement, composed an invitation email, and sent it off to all the contacts I had made since being on the island.

MISSION: The Pacific Island Food Coop on Saipan [will be] a non-profit, member-owned and operated, food cooperative which offers real food (what others call health food) at reasonable prices. We feature non-Genetically modified (Non-GMO), preservative-free, sugar-free, wheat-free, MSG-free, gluten-free, pesticide-free, meat-free, environmentally-friendly, sustainable, organic food, as well as bio-degradable, cruelty-free, recyclable household products from individuals and companies who care about our planet and who share a unique view of real health.

If you share the growing view that real health and wellness doesn't come in the form of factory-made, genetically altered things in boxes or cans, or from pills with multiple side-effects but from a return to what's natural, and if you have certain natural products you'd like to order or see on our shelves, then please complete the registration form below and join with us!

Pool our resources

The strategy is to start first with cooperative purchasing which simply means our members will submit their shopping list, pay in advance and we'll place orders with specific suppliers. As we grow, we'll expand to getting larger and larger shipments and discounts. We intend to pool the power and resources of our growing membership to meet our members' wishes and eventually to be able to negotiate better prices for the products we wish to see here on Saipan. Irene, therefore, will be coordinating the member orders and placing them on a regular basis with our suppliers. She will also be monitoring the growth to help us transition to having our own containers of healthy, organic products shipped directly to our "warehouse."

Involve the local farming community

We believe that our local farmers will be one of our most important allies in helping to offer healthier food to the people of Saipan. We will be spearheading the campaign to introduce alternatives to pesticides, herbicides and other environmentally harmful farming techniques currently in use.

Provide information

We understand that at the basis of all of this is an awareness that one's current dietary choices may not be in one's best interest. For that we need a concerted information campaign to introduce new ideas and dispel old ones, all with a certain degree of cultural sensitivity. For that, the website, the emails and a CD I'll be putting together will introduce some new ideas that people can share with their friends, family and coworkers. Stay tuned!

We believe that given more information, people will make different choices. Walt will be responsible for collecting, compiling and presenting information on alternative products, services, websites, books, programs, etc. for dissemination to membership, media and archiving all of it on our website.

We had our kickoff meeting on September 30th. We placed our first order several days later, and things continue to grow.

Pacific Island Food Co-op founders: Irene, Curt, Lisa, Walt, Franicia, Joe.

Note 37: Guam

Oct 5, 2006

Just came back from Guam! Spent four days and three nights there at the palatial Leo Palace Hotel!

I did a workshop there. My clients were the directors of various departments at the Navy Hospital Guam. The five-day retreat was sponsored by Zita Pangelinan's Pacific Human Resources Company to help the hospital meet some strategic planning objectives. I was the comic relief. No, just kidding. I was there to inject some depth to the concept of harnessing one's passion and unique gifts and channeling them into creating a unique contribution to quality of health care the hospital provides. My workshop kicked of the five-day event.

But let me tell you how I got there. Seems Zita was on Saipan last Wednesday and happened to pick up a copy of the *Saipan Tribune*, which featured my article on Irene Lomosad.

Sensing that my brand of information would fit well with the workshop the Navy Hospital on Guam commissioned her to do, she tracked me down through Joe Hill, and another Pangelinan (Senator Frica), and gave me a call on Friday afternoon.

"I'd like to invite you to Guam to do a workshop," she says.

"When would that take place?" I ask.

"Monday," she replies. (It's now Friday)

"Allrightee, then," I reply.

So, long story short, I agreed, she got me a ticket that same day, and 48 hours later I was on a plane to Guam.

Zita picks me up from the airport, we run a few errands, get acquainted, make some copies for the next day's workshop, and then head to Payless Supermarket, one of the stores that Franicia White (one of the Food Coop's founding members) had told me has some organic, vegetarian selections. What she didn't prepare me for was something that completely blew my mind! We get to payless, and there's an entire section devoted to vegetarian, soy, organic, even vegan food. I don't know if you can make it out in the picture below, but those five banners on the wall read "Vegetarian" "Organic" "Vegan" "Soy" and "Dairy-Free." Now, I mean no disrespect to the consciousness of the other pacific islands, but this is the first time I've seen the word Vegan uttered or displayed by someone other than myself since I've been on this side of the globe! Go Payless!

Happier now than a pig in slop, it gets even better! As I approach the frozen bread section, my heart starts to pound. I catch a glimpse of some familiar colors through the glass door and, as I open it, angels begin to sing, rockets start bursting in air, violins chime in, and a heavenly light emanates from the bottom of the freezer. To my astonishment and elation, Payless Supermarket in Guam carries Ezekiel 4:9 breads and tortillas!

Now that little bit of information may not mean anything to you people, but I had to explain to Zita, the payless management, and a few curious Japanese tourists, why I was doing back flips, salivating and eventually why I purchased all 12 packages of bread to take back to Saipan with me. Only another vegan in this part of the world would understand. In any event, now that Guam has achieved a few brownie points as a possible place for this nomadpreneur to live, I returned to the hotel a happy man.

The next day, I did the workshop.

That's me and my class of diligent military personnel. A great group! Made some friends, too.

Took a little time to see some of the sights on Guam

Goodbye, Guam....Hellooooooo, Saipan!

Once back on Saipan, I quickly proceeded to indulge my proclivities, satiate my pangs of desire, live out my fantasies, gorge myself on the pleasures of my new found paradise by doing that thing that men often do.... *(turn to next page, but brace yourself, and send the children out of the room)*

....yes, you guessed it, I ate myself silly on the twelve packages of Guam-brought, Ezekiel 4:9 bread like it was going out of style!
(sorry, no pictures of me in the act. Some things should remain between a man and his tortilla, after all!)

Note 38: A Week in the Life

Sooooooo.....meanwhile, here on this side of the world, let me see if I can share with you a typical week. After getting up at 6:00 a.m. (4:00 p.m. in the afternoon your time), I'll check emails, have my fulfillment ship orders, and do my website maintenance, write, etc.

Then, by about 10 a.m. or so, pretty much every day, if it's not raining as it has been recently (Typhoon season), I'll ride my bicycle from my part of the island (Chalan Kiya) to Garapan. Usually to Joe-Ten Supermarket to buy a few items to last me 'til the next day. Sometimes I'll stop along Beach road and look out at the Philippine Sea. During the week, the mornings are usually the same, and during the day I'm riding my bicycle running errands, checking my mailbox, meeting clients, interviewing people for my weekly column, perhaps, and writing silly emails to my friends in America.

TUESDAY morning by 11:00 a.m. is my deadline for submitting my column to the Saipan Tribune, so I'm usually inside working up until the last minute.

THURSDAY nights you might find me at The Garapan Street Market (6 p.m. - 9p.m. every Thursday) where local vendors come out and sell mostly cooked food, fruits and vegetables, crafts, and there are usually performances.

FRIDAYS, you might find me at The World Resort Hotel playing table tennis with the guests. Remember, Real Jamaicans say "TT" never "ping pong"!

and then I may head to GIG* for some dancing.

SATURDAY mornings, I usually go to the Sabalu farmer's market.

"Sabalu" is Chamorro for "Saturday."

*[Update] GIG has closed. Perhaps, you'll now find me at The Flair on a Friday night!

At other times you might find me judging a student elocution competition, watching Sam and his kids perform at one of the local spots, or attending a concert.

Sam and family at Bud's Bar in Garapan

One weekend, I found myself participating as a judge in the Renee De Salud Talent Search hosted by Infinity Entertainment and GIG Discotheque.

a prophet's work is never done... at club GIG judging the contestants in the model search competition.

Note 39: Okay, so it's more than a week!

Or you may (but I'd rather you didn't) find me in a secluded spot just sitting and watching the ocean.

Racing around a track

or hanging out with Batman.

Batman???? On Saipan? I guess even caped crusaders need a break from crime-fighting

Note 40: A Few Things I Haven't Done on Saipan

A few things I HAVEN'T done yet, but for which Saipan is known

Cliff Diving

Scuba Diving

I also haven't been snorkeling, horseback riding, parasailing, golfing, banana boating, trekking, skydiving, trolling or, to tell the truth, many of the things there are to do here on this Pacific island tourist destination. Guess, I've just been busy, ok?

Note 41: Heard and Seen on Saipan

Here are a few things you don't hear too often in big cities:

Complete stranger #1 upon first meeting: "Hello. What nationality are you? Where are you from? *(Not an unusual greeting here in this land of many cultures.)*

Complete stranger #2 upon first meeting: "Hey I know you, I've seen you riding your bicycle on Beach Road." *(Ok, so there aren't a lot of people, much less Jamaicans riding bicycles in the heat of the Saipan sun, so I guess I do draw attention. Between the tinted windows, umbrellas, visors, towels and even shrubbery (seen on at least two occasions) that people use to shade themselves from the sun, I get the sense that many people here don't take to the sun as naturally perhaps as this Jamaican does.*

Complete stranger #3 upon first meeting: "Hey I know, you, I've saw you on Tinian." (Tinian is even smaller than Saipan)

Complete stranger #4 as I visited the Sabalu market one day: "Hey brother, the chico, the fruit you like, is over there at that stall." *(Does news travel that fast, and does EVERYONE know what my tastes are? Life in a small town!)*

Joe Hill: "Hey Walt, I heard you were at the Flame Tree Festival yesterday. I also heard you weren't alone." *(Now, hold on just a minute! Isn't anything secret on this little island!?)*

...and some things you don't see

Cultural norms this side of the world require that one take off one's shoes when entering someone's home—a practice I had adopted even while living in New York, but which I failed to impart to the plumbers and electricians who visited my apartment. Anyway, here on Saipan you'll often see multiple pairs of sandals and shoes outside or just inside the doorways of homes. You just don't walk into someone's house with your shoes on!

It's an impressive skill (or perhaps an art to hear some describe it) to witness a woman approaching her home, deftly walking out of her sandals, stepping through the door, in stride, without slowing down, or missing a step, leaving a pair of neatly positioned sandals side by side at the stoop. It's a wonder to behold!

Note 42: My Best Friend's Wedding

Every once in a while, whether through unbridled generosity, overspending, or the giving away of my services, I find myself at a place with limited cash flow, with funds tied up and inaccessible. And, with no credit cards (it's a minimalist thing), I may find myself having to wait for the next royalty check (i.e. the monthly payout from Amazon sales, or online sales to replenish my cash account. *(hey, even Donald Trump has his days, ok?)* The first week of November was one of those times. Now normally, that wouldn't be a huge deal, as my streams of income are pretty reliable. The first week in November was a bit unique, however, in that it was the week Ernest, my best friend in New York, would be getting married—that Saturday in fact. Here's how it went:

TUESDAY

By TUESDAY of the week of Ernest's wedding, I still had not been able to purchase a ticket to fly to New York. I took a look at my bank account, (which hadn't been very cooperative, or inspiring lately) and resigned myself to the very real possibility that I was not going to make it. Bummer, man.

I went online to Continental.com and discovered that a ticket purchased now (three days in advance) would cost $3,000. I called Northwest—the only other airline flying out of Saipan at the time—and got their quote of $2,000. Hmmmm.... this is not good. The funds I was waiting for would only get me up to $1,100, which was what the price of the ticket was two weeks ago. So even if those funds came through, it wouldn't be enough.

So, I called Ernest to tell him the news. He had already figured it out, and mentioned to me that Kim was disappointed that I wouldn't be there. I was, too. I had used all my tricks of visualization and positive expectation, and Jedi mind tricks to will "manna from heaven" to make something happen. But, as I took stock of my cash flow, along with my recent expenses running the company, and starting the food co-op, I realized that even in the best scenario, the funds I awaited would be a day late and a dollar short.

A little bummed out, I called my friend Christie, and then Aaron and Stacey to let them know, too. Yes, it seemed I would miss celebrating the marriage of one of our tight circle of friends.

Well, even though I'd be sad, at least I'd have life in Sunny Saipan to console me.

WEDNESDAY

So, on WEDNESDAY, with no apparent need to save every penny for a plane ticket, I decided to treat myself to a few items I'd been holding off on purchasing, and went shopping. As I was driving up Monsignor Guerrero Road on my way from one of the shops, I had a thought!

It occurred to me that if you want to take a train, you go to the train station and pay your fare. If you want to take a bus, you go to the bus terminal and buy a ticket. So, I reasoned, if I want to take a plane, what better place to go than....you guessed it, the airport!

So, I drove to the Saipan International Airport, parked and took a walk upstairs to the administrative offices of the individual airlines. First stop: the Continental airline office. I asked about flights to NY, but got the same information I had gotten online.

"Well, how about a one-way ticket?" I asked the agent.

"$1,500," she replied after a quick search.

"Hmmmm. Ok. Let's do it," I said.

And so I reserved a one-way ticket on Continental for $1,500. I figured getting there was more important. By the time I got there, book sales and internet income would have accumulated, and/or I could always make something happen and buy a return ticket for whatever it cost, once I got there.

But I wasn't done yet. (Continental was actually my plan B). My next stop was the Northwest Airlines office. I had dealt with Northwest before, on my last trip. (If you recall, Northwest was my airline of choice for my first Escape from America; So I have warm spot in my heart for NWA.)

At the Northwest office, I met Esther, the same young lady I had dealt with before.

Esther at the Northwest Airlines Office

"Esther," I told her, "my best friend is getting married in NY on Saturday, and I have to find a way to get there!"

She raised her eyebrows as she looked at her screen and started typing. She looked up the information and said, "Well, Mr. Goodridge, a one-way ticket is $2,000. Normally, it would be less, but that would require a 14-day advance purchase."

"Well, Esther, don't you have the magical power to sort of like, waive that pesky little requirement?" I asked coyly.

She didn't answer, punched some more keys, then punched even more keys, and then said, "I can get you a flight for $1100," she said.

"OK, but just curious, how much would a round-trip cost?"

"That IS a round-trip," she replied. Since it's your best friend's wedding, I'll waive the 14-day requirement for you. But just this one time."

Great! I love Saipan! I thought. It's never over 'til it's over! I could feel that old familiar last minute, eleventh hour, stroke of midnight, make-it-happen feeling stirring—the kind of feeling that always comes before a great story! With the price of the ticket now within reach, all I needed was a little help from my friends to make this happen. Yep, I'll get by (again) with a little help from my friends!

It was 3:00 in the afternoon. (That would be 12:00 a.m. the stroke of midnight in the wee hours of the morning New York time), so I called Stacey (mother of two who, I am sure just LOVES these early morning calls) to let her know that I was working on making something happen, and that I might need her help in a few hours!

Meanwhile, Esther grants me 24 hours to come back with the payment. She says I have to be back before 6:00 p.m. the next day—Thursday—to pay for the ticket.

Just so you're clear, the Friday morning flight Esther just booked me on is the last possible flight I can take leaving Saipan to reach NY in enough time to make the wedding. It gets into NY at 2:00 p.m. on Friday afternoon. (FYI: Saipan is 15 hours ahead of NY; so I can leave on Friday—Saipan time—travel almost a full day, and I arrive on the same day NY time!)

I drive back home, compose and send an email to seven of my "best" friends. *(i.e. the friends with enough normalcy and stability in their lives to be able to help last-minute, spontaneous, impetuous nomads like me!)* p.s. If you weren't one of them, don't worry, it doesn't mean you're not stable, it just means I wanted to surprise you too! hee hee)

Within ten minutes of sending the email (1:00 a.m. EST), my friend Andrew Paypal's me $100. A few hours later, Monica sends $150, then Pramod sends me $100 (with a note chastising me for being unstable, abnormal, spontaneous and impetuous), and later that evening, Stacey's $400 comes through! A few orders for my books come through the website, and whaddya know, I'm good to go! Life is great! That night, I headed to Saipan's only movie theatre and treated myself to *Jackass 2*, the movie.

THURSDAY:
The next day, THURSDAY, I run some errands until 2:30 p.m., and then head to the airport, and head upstairs to pay for my ticket.

Esther is waiting for me. I split the cost of the ticket between cash and my debit card, get my ticket in hand, (all in less than 24 hours after thinking my "no-show" was a done-deal), smile and think to myself: *Why can't my life be like normal folks?*

Anyhoo, that's how it all happened! And how I made it to New York for Ernest's wedding!

EPILOGUE:
At 9:00 p.m. that Thursday night, three hours *after* the ticket offices at the airport closed for the day—three short hours past the deadline to purchase a ticket on the latest possible flight out of Saipan, a chunk of money I'd been waiting for since April shows up in my account! It was more than enough to cover what I needed for the ticket, and by extension, all the loans I had just received. (How frustrating would THAT have been if, instead of going to the airport, I had simply come straight home on that fateful Wednesday and then discovered on Thursday night that I had enough money to buy the ticket, but it was too late to do so???)

p.s. Even though I like to tell a suspenseful story, the moment I had the idea to go to the airport that Wednesday is when I knew that the tide of circumstance had shifted, and that I would, despite all evidence to the contrary, be in NY.... for my best friend's wedding!

Jamaican On Saipan! 117

Me and the "Table 12" Crew at Ernest and Kim's wedding in New York.

*The "Briarwood Seven" plus Kim and Ernest.
Friends for life! (or at least until we start fighting over money!)*

    This trip to see Ernest's and Kim's wedding was only about two weeks. I had to get back to spend....

Note 43: The Holidays on Saipan

my first Thanksgiving...

The Chinese, Filipino, American, Japanese, Chamorro, Carolinian, Nigerian, Ghanaian and Jamaican friends at Joe Hill's house for his annual Thanksgiving day event.

And Christmas...

Picture-taking on the Paseo de Marianas

Jamaican On Saipan! 119

and Kwanzaa....yes, I said Kwanzaa on Saipan!

Children from Whispering Palms School explain the Nguzo Saba to a rapt audience.

Rose Smith (with microphone), Saipan's only (I think) Kenyan, explains the significance of the principles of Kwanzaa to a packed house at the Multi-Purpose Center in Susupe.

And this is where I was and what I was doing on New Year's day on Saipan. How 'bout you?

Forbidden Island, one of my favorite spots to take visitors

Saipan on the rocks!

Note 44: Beautify C.N.M.I

Volunteers pick up trash around the island.

    A great phenomenon taking place on Saipan is the BeautifyCNMI movement. BeautifyCNMI is a coalition of concerned citizens, private groups, and government entities united to enhance the CNMI's natural beauty and foster community pride in its residents and visitors. (www.BeautifyCNMI.com).

    It all started from Cinta Kaipat's vision fueled by her passion and love for her home, family and community. It found a catalyst at a meeting in June of 2006, at what was then called The Beautification Group, which had started meeting a month earlier.

    From a humble tree-planting event, the small group of core volunteers, which eventually became Beautify CNMI has achieved an impressive record: 2,000 trees have been planted since June; 260,000 lbs of recyclable material have been collected in just two months; 3,380 volunteers showed up for the island-wide cleanup on Oct 20, 2006.

    Beautify CNMI is galvanizing the community in a way that's never been done. Chamorros, Carolinians, Filipinos, Chinese, Koreans, Japanese, and many others are all uniting every week with a common goal.

The next big long-term project is The Micronesia Challenge. (The "challenge," first proposed by Palau President Tommy Remengesau Jr., and taken up by the leaders of the CNMI, Guam, Marshall Islands, and Federated States of Micronesia, is to "effectively conserve 30% of "near shore" resources, 20% of forest resources" by 2020.) Beautify CNMI!'s mission is to get the vision of this challenge into the heads and hearts of the everyone.

"We have more coral reefs than any place in the world," Angelo offers. "So when this challenge is successful we will have protected larger swaths of reef than any other. We can be the shining star of Micronesia in that regard. The CNMI can, should and will be THE place for people to witness and experience coral reef conservation in action. The CNMI also can, should and will be known for industries, opportunities and based on our natural resources.

"What I love about Beautify CNMI is that it embodies a traditionally independent spirit and a belief that we are self-sufficient and that we CAN do it ourselves. Help from the outside can supplement, but we really should strive to be helping ourselves. The success of Beautify CNMI! shows that we're ready and that we ARE doing it!"

"I also love the diverse and beautiful people on Saipan. Take a walk through the Thursday Night Street Market and you are bound to overhear conversations in Chamorro, Carolinian, English, Tagalog, Japanese, Chinese, Korean, Russian, and a dozen other languages. No other place this size has so much diversity.

--Angelo Villagomez, (from an interview I did for the Tribune)

Note: BeautifyCNMI received the Saipan Tribune's Person of the Year award.

Note 45: WeLoveSaipan

Before coming to Saipan, I did a little of my own research on the internet, and found that there was not much about Saipan that was of the tone and timbre that Ken expressed when he first told me about it. I realized, as I met more people whose life paths carried them here, that their perceptions were being skewed by one site in particular which was excessively negative about life here. I decided to do something about it.

I reserved the WeLoveSaipan.com domain name, and then recruited the assistance of Angelo Villagomez, a local blogger with Saipan's most popular blog to help me publicize it.

I launched the site on Dec 6, 2006, with the express purpose of countering the negative image that people might receive. Angelo mentioned it on his blog. He came up with the idea of creating a button that other bloggers could easily put on their sites linking to us. I mentioned it in my weekly article. We listed it on various search engines and directories. I set up a link program which allowed others to find and link to us, thus increasing our ranking. We both monitored the site, doing searches on Google and seeing how our efforts were being rewarded. If you did a search for "Saipan" on the day we launched, you'd have had to scroll through 15 pages of listings to find us at position 155. Within a few weeks we were at position 120, then 100. We were amazed to see how quickly we were moving up the search results. Our network grew, more bloggers added links to us, we got encouragement and support from senators, congresswomen, attorneys, even an assistant attorney general with a blog chimed in! On April 4, 2007, almost exactly four months from launch, I sent the following email:

Dear WeLoveSaipan Network Member,
    OK, folks, this is the email I've been anxiously waiting to send for a while now....

(drum roll please)....

As of April 4, 2007, at 7:58 p.m. Chamorro Standard Time (ChST), approximately 120 days from initial launch on December 6, 2006, the WeLoveSaipan.com site now appears on the first page (Top 10!) of listings for the first time ever on a Google.com search for "Saipan!"

This has been no easy feat and represents the combined efforts, mental energies, visualizations, positive expectations and support of the entire WeLoveSaipan network!

Now, keep in mind that your search results may vary slightly as there are fluctuations in search engine results depending on time of day, browser used, etc. This position represents a continuing climb in rank that has proceeded unabated for the past 4 months, and is the beginning of some great things about to happen.

What this means for the site and for Saipan is that more people will discover what life is like here through our combined positive perspectives as many people often don't venture past the first page of listings for any search.

It means we've proven that it is possible to affect search engine ranking with a little creativity and no money. (Ok, maybe only the techies care about that one!)

What this means for YOU is that your link on our site will potentially be viewed by many more people and drive visitors to your blog.

In any event, though there may be no headline announcements in tomorrow's paper, trust me, the significance of what we, "The Official Network of Saipan Bloggers", has accomplished can no longer be denied!!!!! Um...ok, got a little carried away there...

Anyway, have a great day!

Walt

p.s. Depending if and when you do the search to see it for yourself, you may also notice that certain "other" sites have mysteriously disappeared from their top ten spot. Yes, Angelo and I can do magic with our minds!

Note 46: The Master Plan

Shortly after I sent that email, Gus Kaipat of Saipan's Olomwaay Band emailed me.

 How can we make the rest of the world care?

My reply: (which I promptly sent to the entire network):
Ahhhh....that's the easy part, my friend...And that's where the Master Plan can now be revealed! (I know it's a bit lengthy, but it is a master plan, after all). You get the rest of the world to care by doing a few things...

1. Change the dialogue
Right now, because of what we're doing, there's a new dialogue developing. Angelo received this comment on his site:
"My father lives on Saipan and I was just looking through the net for information regarding the Tsunami. Little did I know that I would have the opportunity to review your page. It is wonderful, the pictures fantastic, and your involvement in the beautification of the islands is commendable. Very nice! Thanks for the opportunity.

There are an increasing number of people around the world who, after now discovering us through these new channels, are saying things like:
"I'm thinking of moving to Saipan!"
"Have you ever heard of a place called Saipan?
"Ever thought about retiring on Saipan?"
The dialogue is changing.

2. Create a different story to tell
Once the dialogue is begun, you give people a different story to tell. If you remember from my workshop, people are moved to action by either fun, facts, help(the desire to help others) or money. The new stories we can tell through our blogs and our internet presence can provide information that appeals to those who want more FACTS about life on Saipan, those who relate to the desire to HELP others, those who want to have FUN, and those who want to make MONEY.

So the dialogue continues like this
"No? Well it's this little island in the Pacific..."

"Yeah, Saipan....Apparently it's like this little paradise island where people are going to retire, start their own business or just get away from the rat race!"

"Really? How come I never heard about it?"

"I dunno, but....check out the welovesaipan.com site. It shows what life is really like from the perspectives of a group of bloggers who live there, and they got their site in the top ten listings in 3 months! (facts)

"Check out beautifycnmi.com. Volunteers got together to clean up the island and improve life on the island... (help)

"Check out thesaipanblogger.com. There's this guy named Angelo who has a fun site about life on Saipan (fun)

"Check out passionprofit.com, there's even this one author who just picked up and moved there to escape from America and started this thing called the Saipanpreneur project to help people start their own businesses. (money)

3. Instill pride in our own people

It's not enough to change the external dialogue, it's even more important to change the internal dialogue. Franicia's not the first person I heard say she was told "tell them you're from Hawaii." She writes:

"On a personal note, I just want to thank all of you for the work you put into the island especially this site, especially to Walt and Angelo. I remember when I left for college and people would tell me that it was easier to just say that I was from Hawaii. "Why bother explaining to them where Saipan is?" I thought the idea was crazy. Why lie? Why Hawaii? I've always loved my home. I loved talking about Saipan so much that I didn't mind having a hard time explaining more about it. Thank you all for helping keep the island beautiful."

I've met people who DID and DO in fact tell others they're from Hawaii. But, NOW, if there's a different dialogue, something people can be proud of, then the dialogue can change to:

"YEAH, I'm from Saipan! Not Taipei, you idiot, SAIPAN! "I don't know why you never heard of it, maybe you've been living under a rock! Check out WeloveSaipan.com or BeautifyCNMI.com and get yourself educated!"

Or, as stories circulate, they may start to hear things like *"oooh, I hear you're from Saipan! I saw Angelo's website! Is it REALLY like that over there?"*
"oh, yeah, Saipan....isn't that that island where.....[fill in the blank]"

4. Balance the new person's experience

The power of the #10 or front page spot is that from now on whenever ANYONE seeks information about SAIPAN, we'll be there. The stories on the WeloveSaipan.com site are a permanent fixture on the internet which will henceforth flavor almost everyone's introduction to the CNMI. These days, people who want to learn about a new place, person or thing, go straight for the computer, the internet, and 50% of them, I'm told use Google specifically.

With our #10 position (and rising), and with the "disappearance" and increasing inconsistency of that "other" site, which up until now had been a fixture of a negative nature, we have taken control of what that experience will be.

Let me repeat: WE ARE IN CONTROL OF WHAT A NEW PERSON'S EXPERIENCE OF SAIPAN WILL BE.

Now, even if that "other" site appears, and even if it continues to exist. It is now outnumbered by other positive sites, so people will recognize it for what it is: just one person's vitriolic opinion in a sea of love, and they can judge it accordingly. To give you an example of what I mean, one of the people who responded to my post on the www.early-retirement.org forum did his own search for Saipan, found that "other" site and said "It seems that Saipan is a beautiful little island, but there may be a few flies in the ointment..."

Think about that for a second.

When he says, *"It seems that Saipan is a beautiful little island,"* that comes from him having seen welovesaipan, my site, and Angelo's blog...

When he says, *"there may be a few flies in the ointment,"* that comes from what he read on that "other" site

Now, as much as I wish that other site didn't exist, keep in mind that he found it AFTER reading the welovesaipan.com site, so his phrase to describe it ("flies in the ointment") came out a a whole lot more balanced than if that "other" site were his only source of information. That, my friend, is what this is all about.

5. Do your thing

Bloggers are sharing their Why I Love Saipan testimonials and lifestyles in their blogs. Gus is creating music for the world. Cinta is pushing for legislation to make life better here; Angelo is creating Tsunami documentaries of 2 mm high waves and sticking boarding passes to his forehead; Walt is singing Saipan's praises on his business blog and forums; Steve is helping the mentally ill; Everyone's got their "thing."

So, THAT'S how we make the rest of the world care, Gus. We just continue to do our thing, and the people, the pride, the power and the position will attract the attention of kindred spirits who want a new story to tell, or to be a part of it all....

One of my all-time favorite photos taken on Saipan! The Chamorro, Filipino, Iranian, Korean, Vietnamese, American, Japanese, Russian, Canadian and Jamaican bloggers at the Blogger Meetup on Saipan.

Note 47: How We REALLY Did It

Yes, we were able to accomplish something really special. Yep, it's pretty cool....But now for the real cool part....

On a metaphysical level, I believe in the power of thought to activate unseen forces and mobilize them to assist in the manifestation of positive, worthy causes, intentions and goals.

It is a basic function of the world that I choose to live in that every call is answered, every knock is responded to, and every wish is granted. If it doesn't always seem that way, it's because we see the often necessary DEconstruction that must precede REconstruction of a new reality as a negative thing, and then abandon our dreams before they form.

Having all of us, or at least you and me, Angelo, focusing our thought energies, on a daily basis, visualizing our outcome can not be discounted as the REAL reason this is taking place. Those with the power to create, do so through thought alone. Reality, physical objects, people's behavior, and the simple stuff like the inner workings of the Google search engine algorithm, bend to the will of those with vision.

I have a mantra on my wall that reads:
My Greatness Manifests...
By Thought Alone...
In the Service of Other Selves...
By Seeking Always the Affirmative
Use of All Apparent Limitations

The "limitation" of Saipan's previous online presence, and dearth of empowering images and stories of life here, before you came along was turned into a positive through TheSaipanBlogger.com, BeautifyCNMI.com, and now WeLoveSaipan.com, which all provide benefit and service to others!

The intention of what we wish to achieve is what registers with the universe, polarizes us towards service to others, and by natural law makes miracles--or, at least what some would perceive as such. But should one really expect anything less than miracles in paradise?

Note 48: MLK Day in the CNMI

Back in April 2006, Governor Fitial signed the bill proclaiming Martin Luther King Jr Day as a CNMI-wide holiday. On January 17 of 2007, thanks to the collaboration of a coalition of organizations and individuals spearheaded by the African American Cultural Preservation Committee here on Saipan, we had our first observance here. After weeks of planning, we had an Essay and Elocution Contest, a civil rights march through the streets of Saipan, performances, and a guest speaker flown in from Arkansas.

With the Junior ROTC Honor Guard leading the way....

and a banner proclaiming the history-making event...

Jamaican On Saipan! 131

... they took to the streets of Garapan in true civil rights movement style!

Meanwhile, we judged the essays for the MLK Essay & Elocution Contest!

And Ranger Nancy prepared the top cop for the evening ceremony!

Dr. Cynthia Nance of the University of Arkansas tells it like it was!

But this was no ordinary guest speaker. Saipan was fortunate to have as the keynote speaker of our inaugural MLK day event, Dean Cynthia Nance. Here is an excerpt from a letter crafted by Joe Hill seeking sponsorship and support for the event:

Dean Cynthia E. Nance is the first woman and first black dean of the University of Arkansas at Fayetteville, Law School, and is a Professor of law.

To place Dean/Professor Nance's accomplishments in perspective, it should be known that Arkansas is where Governor Orval Fabus, in 1957, in defiance of the orders of President Eisenhower to admit black students to Little Rock Central High School and in the face of the National Guard, and in the eyes of the world, vowed publicly that black and white children would never be allowed to attend school together in the State of Arkansas. Dean/Professor Nance, in the true spirit of Dr. King's dream, has "over come" such entrenched barriers of racial discrimination in education and employment opportunities, and her professional and academic achievements serve as an inspiration to freedom loving people everywhere. [end]

My friend Joe Hill is fond of saying Saipan is truly where east meets west. The unique mix of Asian and American influence along with other ethnic and cultural experiences, world views and perspectives makes life here an object lesson in harmony. It's been described as "better than a melting pot" where each of the dozens of unique cultures remains intact while co-existing right next door to each other. Perhaps Martin Luther King Jr. would be proud.

Note 49: Early-Retirement on Saipan

Keeping in Touch
    I recently came across a web forum at early-retirement.org, a community of individuals devoted to freeing themselves as early as possible from the rat race, and helping others do the same. That concept, as you can imagine is one dear to my heart having "retired" from corporate employment back in 1995. When I found the site, I decided to register and offer myself as a resource.
    Little did I know just how popular that message board was! Within about 2 minutes, several people had viewed my "From a "retired" nomadpreneur on a Pacific island" posting and a flurry of communication began. Soon, the thread got around to inquiries about Saipan, and escapes to paradise, and I recommended checking out WELOVESAIPAN.com. One member asked how I dealt with losing touch with friends and family back in the states.
    I replied: Now, I can only speak from my personal experience, but what I've found is I actually speak to some of my friends MORE now than I did when I was in New York. Being caught up in the pressures and pace of day-to-day life in the big city made it almost impossible to really hang out with friends to any satisfying degree. Everyone had jobs, appointments, play dates, and errands to run. And being the only one of my friends with control of my days, I was pretty much isolated. Even my other entrepreneur friends were too busy, having set up systems that required their constant presence. We communicated mostly by phone and email. So, the truth is, even though I'm now 8,000 miles away, I don't really see my friends any less than I did when I was there. (Keep in mind, however, I've always been a loner, so my need for social interaction may be a bit less than yours.)
    Now, from another perspective, I'd like to suggest that you don't really LOSE anything or anyone by moving to paradise and living your dream. There are so many new people, new ways to be, new realities and new perspectives to grow into by having the courage to live life on your terms, that I believe you actually do yourself more of a disservice by NOT expanding your social, emotional and spiritual circles with an excursion into your private paradise. The urge you feel, and the call that you hear is your higher self summoning you to expand.
    In this deeper sense, if you can appreciate the spiritual nature of your being, you are never, ever truly separated from

anyone. It's your belief in separateness that keeps you bound. And while admittedly, physical proximity has its benefits, the real connection and bond with friends and family is one that occurs on a non-physical level. Such a bond can only be enhanced once you grow into a person who has the courage to live his dreams. You'll become more of the you you were meant to be, and as a result you'll be a better uncle, father, brother and son, as well as a true inspiration for those who love you and whom you love. Just think how your conversations with them, and the advice you can give them will be radically altered when you take the leap!

At the same time, as you grow and expand, you'll necessarily lose touch with others, not because you're far away physically, but because you'll be traveling psychologically to new lands. It's bound to happen. Personally, I think the bigger fear many people have is not losing PHYSICAL touch with those they call friend/family, but losing psychological touch when all those they know are choosing to live "lesser-than lives" while they graduate to live lives of passion.

No, my early-retirement friend, the "problem" is not how to handle the distance between bodies, the challenge is how to handle the distance between minds that a life in paradise often brings.

But, you have an obligation to yourself, your dreams and your own happiness. Your friends and family are choosing to living their lives. You should live yours, too.

Walt

On a practical note, Saipan is a US commonwealth, so a long distance call from the states to here is the same as dialing any other state, so there's no added expense. Cell phones, email, blogs, Skype, et.al. are great ways to keep in touch.

Note 50: Island Fever?

Another member of the early-retirement network asked about dealing with "island fever" which he described as "a variation of Cabin Fever for residents in snowy climates, and is the desire to hop in your car and drive in a straight line for 500 miles."
I replied:
LOL. I guess you might indeed experience Island Fever here, as Saipan (at 12.5 miles x 5.5 miles; 46sq miles) is a lot smaller even than Jamaica (4,411 square miles) where I grew up.

But I guess it boils down to what you're accustomed to. I recall friends in the states asking me if sunshine year-round growing up didn't get boring after a while. Being from an island where warm weather is the 365-24-7 norm (except for the occasional hurricane), you accept it as just the way it is. One's "excitement" doesn't hinge on the appearance of falling leaves, snowflakes or radical fluctuations in temperature. And "isolation" isn't a function of the size or the seasons, but something else entirely.

While living in Manhattan, I guess you could say I suffered from "city fever", which I would define as "the desire to step out my door and interact in more socially meaningful, spiritually uplifting and physically nourishing ways with people and nature."

Living in the big city, I felt more isolated in my fifth floor apartment where I could live for years and never meet my next-door neighbor, where I could leave my apartment at the same time each day but never see the same person twice, where I could stand in a subway car, wedged body-to-body against another human being and never make eye contact, or acknowledge their existence, and where the interactions I did have were typically hurried, stress-laden, and perfunctory in nature.

But that's not to disparage New York, or any big city. There is a reality of human interaction that occurs in any environment where people are forced to reside in unnatural numbers. I recall reading an article that talked about the psychological necessity of shutting down after a while when one encounters so many people every second of the day. Acting on your natural impulse to smile, acknowledge or greet every single person you encounter would drive you crazy, or simply brand you as such.

So the emotional distance and detachment that often attends life in a million-man metropolis is a survival mechanism.

Here on Saipan, however, you can't pass another human without some acknowledgment that a life form is in your presence. It would be considered rude. People smile, say hello, and some will even call and wave to you from across the street! (Not everyone, of course....you can usually tell the tourists or the newbies on the island, as they're the ones who often don't, retaining as they do their mode of social interaction from whence they cometh... until they warm up a bit.) Even after being here a while, it still makes me smile inside and out when it happens! I hear it's even friendlier on neighboring islands where outside influence is even less.

The ability to connect with others is what defines MY sense of isolation. And although I too love a good long early morning drive on a long highway, (I used to head from Maryland to Atlanta and do the whole ten-hour drive in one sitting), given the choice, I'll opt for
> *short dirt roads and friendly smiles,*
> *over frowns and streets that run for miles....*

After directing my new acquaintances to the welovesaipan.com site, I received the following:

"I am very impressed. I never thought of early retiring there until seeing this website. I am interested in finding out more."--Jim W (from the early-retirement.org forum) [end of email]

and

Hello, Walt!
I've just ordered two of your books. You've done a wonderful job achieving freedom. I'm a doctor, and I've been contacted by CHC [Commonwealth Health Center—Saipan's hospital] in Saipan to join their staff. I'm seriously considering it. I'm also a direct marketer, one-on-one student of Dan Kennedy and fan of Mark Joyner, Joe Vitale, and many others you may know (I'm guessing from your marketing style). I hope to get to Saipan at least to check out the sweet life, and hopefully to move there with my family! All the best,
Marc S., M.D. Norfolk, VA, USA [end of email]

Ahhhh, yes. My work here is done!

Gratuitous beach scene to remind you where I am: Saipan!

Note 51: Saipan Calling!

My experience here is not unique. Many people who visit Saipan rave about its native beauty, the warmth of its people, and the multiculturalism. There's probably no better place one can come to learn a host of different languages, interact with unique cultures, and experience a tolerance and slower pace of life, while basking in trade winds and sunshine.

There are challenges here to be sure, and like any place you go in life, you often find what you're looking for, what you believe, and what you expect. Should you ever decide to visit this little corner of the world, come with an open mind, and leave your expectations behind.

In truth, my "work" is far from done. As I've said earlier, I've accepted that my life is a story to be told, and that in the telling there may be information, inspiration or ideas others can use to grow. If, while being personally blessed with an experience that fulfills my own dreams, I can share that experience with the world and help in some small way to improve life here, encourage others to see themselves and their world a little differently, find the courage to live their own dreams and then venture out beyond the boundaries of thought and experience that keep them bound, then I can say I've been successful.

Many people are impressed, intrigued, and even incensed by my decision to pick up and trek to the other side of the world in search of happiness. In truth, my journey is no different from any leap of faith that one is often required to take in pursuit of his or her own world.

A few months ago, while talking to a friend and her daughter in NY from here on Saipan, I mentioned that Saipan is fifteen hours ahead of New York Eastern Standard Time. So while it was 9:00 p.m. on Tuesday in New York, it was 12:00 noon on *Wednesday* on Saipan. My friend's daughter said she couldn't wait to tell her friends at school that she knew "someone from the future!" It was an innocent, yet profound comment (thanks, Kai), one that inspired the following life rhyme:

Note 52: Someone from the Future!

It's just a different time zone
hmmm, but wait, perhaps it's more
It just might have the makings
of the perfect metaphor

For time zones are like comfort zones
one journeys to break free
And once you do you'll live a different world
that most won't see

And calendars and clocks
are just a construct we impose
Just others' expectations
of a world led by the nose

Walt's Life Rhyme #445
Someone From The Future

And sunrises like dreams
are what you see while others sleep
And sunsets here in paradise
are scenes that most won't reap

Yes, someone from the future called
it's you your dream sublime
And anyone can take the leap
sail forward anytime

It need not be an island dream
found halfway 'round the earth
The future's any place
your actions to your dreams give birth!

For me Saipan is a real place. For you, if nothing else, let it be a metaphor for your journey, your own happiness, your own world.

    See you in, or on Saipan!!

Jamaican on Saipan! TWO

Reloaded!
The Sequel!
Revisited!
Part II!

The Story Continues!

It is now February 23, 2010—exactly four years since touching down on Saipan. In the time I've been here, much has happened. I continue to write my weekly column for the Saipan Tribune. I received a senate resolution recognizing my contributions to the CNMI. I've seen two more MLK Day celebrations. My father passed away. Barack Obama has been elected president of the US. The last garment factory on Saipan has closed. I've helped a Chinese garment factory worker write her memoirs. The Mariana Trench Marine National Monument has been created. And, by the time you read this, a new book and site—*Doing Business on Saipan* should be launched. But let me take it all one step at a time…

Note 53: There's always something to do on Saipan!

Here are a few of the activities I've been involved in.

Dedication and Grand opening ceremony for the Kagman Wetlands Conservation Project

Judging students' science projects

An American couple living in Japan contacted me through the WeLoveSaipan.com site re: finding authentic Shinto shrines outside of Japan. Saipan happens to be one of those rare locations as a result of the Japanese presence prior to and up to World War II. I offered to take them around to see one of the shrines on Saipan. There were also World War II shells, ammunition, canteens and more to touch and photograph.

One of the few Shinto Shrines outside of Japan

Taking photos of actual WW II shells.

Meeting visiting diplomats and politicians

Had a chance to meet with Dirk Kempthorne, US Secretary of Interior (holding beautify CNMI t-shirt), on his visit to Saipan. He commented on my Thailand style shirt with the elephant on it. I didn't make the connection (Elephant=Republican symbot) until later. You don't think he thought I was....? Naw!

...and going dancing whenever the mood strikes.

Jamaican On Saipan! 143

I joined a co-ed league and did one season of soccer!

Had to represent Jamaican ballers here in the Pacific!

The Food Co-op meets occasionally to purchase, or share recipes.

Food Co-op members Lisa and Dorothea at the kitchen at Northern Marianas College (NMC)

I meet new and interesting people from strange, exotic ports, or is that strange, exotic people from…..? Anyway…

My buddy, Captain Ian Mayne, and crew on a visit to Saipan

And, of course, I do my part to help the tourism industry! (Hey, someone has to!)

I'm now convinced that the "peace" sign is mandated by law for all Japanese tourists whenever they pose for photos.

From Russia: One Love. She played pretty well for her first time!

I grow my own wheatgrass

My tray of wheat grass

And I still go where the sun is shining to soak it all in!

Note 54: The Best of Saipan!

Okay. I've been here long enough now to make some serious observations and do something worthwhile for the community. Since I actually enjoy creating websites, I've focused on creating a suite of sites to cover as many aspects of life on Saipan as possible. As of February 2010, I've launched the following websites for Saipan, with more on the way!

WeLoveSaipan.com
A new perspective from the network of Saipan bloggers!

DiscoverSaipan.com
Offering Walt's special tour of Saipan!

Saipanpreneur.com
Encouraging entrepreneurship in the CNMI

Saipanliving.com
See what it's like to live on an island paradise.

SaipanCrafts.com
Unique handcrafts from Saipan.

BlacksonSaipan.com
A blog for the African American Cultural Preservation Committee on Saipan; Joe Hill, President

SaipanFactoryGirl.com (also on Facebook® and Youtube®)
The site for the book, Chicken Feathers and Garlic Skin: Diary of a Chinese Garment Factory Girl on Saipan

TheNewSaipan.com
A collection of my articles, essays and thoughts on re-branding Saipan and reviving the Saipan economy.

DestinationSaipan.com
Your portal to Paradise; Accommodations and tours!

Visit www.bestofsaipan.com to see how the network grows.

Note 55: My Senate Resolution!

A lot of what I've been doing has come to the attention of the movers and shakers on Capitol Hill. On December 12, 2007, I was the honored recipient of CNMI Senate Resolution NO. 15-54, entitled "*A Senate Resolution congratulating Mr. Walt Frederick Jerome Goodridge on his numerous accomplishments within and without the Commonwealth; expressing gratitude for his efforts for the betterment of the people of the Commonwealth; wishing him success in all his future endeavors.*"

It was introduced by Senator Pete P. Reyes. The resolution hangs proudly on my wall at home.

Picture on the Wall

Note 56: Contract Workers Unite

Big news here on Saipan was the recent march and rally for and by contract workers who are seeking improved immigration status here in the CNMI.

Contract worker rally at American Memorial Park

Note 57: Another Jamaican!

Jamaican, Cardiff Walker is a pilot for Freedom Air.

Note 58: MLK Day Traditions Continue!

I wasn't actually on Saipan for the January 2008, celebration as I was in New York, but I was here for the 2009. This year's keynote speaker was MarshaRose Joyner, an activist in Hawaii with a rich history of agitation! The MLK day traditions continue with our mini-march, MLK Day essay contest...

This year's guest speaker MarshaRose Joyner and the winners of the Essay and Elocution Contest. This year's theme: What Would Martin Say?

...and the tradition of me taking our guest speaker to see some of Saipan's sights!

Marsha Rose Joyner at Mount Tapochau! (Read Marsha Rose's unique connection to Saipan and why we chose her as keynote speaker at www.blacksonsaipan.com)

Note 59: Food for a Week on Saipan!

Here on Saipan, I live a simple life. I don't drink. I don't smoke. I'm vegan. I eat very few things that are packaged or bottled. I drink only coconut water and bottled water. While surfing the internet, I was inspired by a photo essay from a book entitled *Hungry Planet* by Peter Menzel and Faith D'Aluisio which detailed what people eat and spend on their weekly sustenance in different countries and cultures.

I was inspired to create my own, and so, having entirely too much time on my hands, I created this to add to the email I sent to my friends about the book and online photo essay:

Saipan: *The Jamaican Vegan on Saipan Chalan Kiya*
Food expenditure for one week: about $75 US (usually less)
Favorites: coconut water, sapodillas, Ezekiel™ bread, Lara™ bars
Paradise is easy if your needs are few.

Note 60: Marianas Trench Marine National Monument

On Tuesday January 6, 2009, former President Bush designated three new marine national monuments in the Pacific Ocean that total an area of more than 195,561 square miles in size. When added with the already established Papahānaumokuākea Marine National Monument, former President Bush will have designated monuments protecting 335,358 square miles — larger than the entire U.S. National Park system, and more than double the area of U.S. ocean now protected.

The Mariana Trench and Islands – discovered by Ferdinand Magellan and located in the far western Pacific this U.S. position is the site of the Mariana Trench, at 36,000 feet, the deepest canyon on the globe. If Mt. Everest were dropped into the Trench, there would still be more than a mile of water above it.

More than 95,000 sq. miles in area, this monument protects some of the most diverse and remarkable underwater features on the globe. Features of the Mariana region include a boiling pool of liquid sulfur (the first pool was discovered on Io, one of Jupiter's moons), liquid carbon dioxide that bubbles up through fractured lava, and dense beds of chemosynthetic life covering submarine crater walls. The area represents the only place on Earth with huge, active mud volcanoes, one more than 31 miles across. These unusual features are believed to harbor some of the oldest known life on the DNA tree.....[from globaloceanlegacy.org]

Senior Bush advisor James Connaughton comes to visit

...and is welcomed by the army of orange-t-shirt sporting, button-wearing, banner-carrying tree huggers on Saipan!

That's what the world hears about the monument. The whole process of educating the public, seeking support of the monument and eventually passage of the act took place between Saipan and Washington DC.

What the world *didn't* see was all the drama on this side of the ocean here on Saipan. Here in the CNMI, it was front page news, and the talk of many who live here for months and months. The Pew Environment group, which proposed the creation of the monument became the catalyst for a story made for the big screen. The proposal created an "us and them" battle of sorts among the residents of the community, with people fearing the CNMI was giving up ownership of the islands, others fearing fishing rights would be lost, and others maintaining that the natural resources should be conserved, protected, and that the designation would result in untold positive media exposure and financial benefit to Saipan. The highest levels of government opposed it, the public supported it, tensions flared, letter writing campaigns proliferated, misinformation abounded, bloggers blustered, petitions were passed around (200 local businesses and 6,000 citizens signed petitions in support), there was name-calling and finger-pointing galore!

Pew Charitable Trusts was on-site, James Connaughton (chair of the White House Council on Environmental Quality and senior advisor to Bush) came to visit, Laura Bush gave her support, Dick Cheney opposed it, the local opposition capitulated, President Bush passed the act, the world's attention is turning, and now everyone wants to take credit! And it all happened here on Saipan! Wish you could have been here!

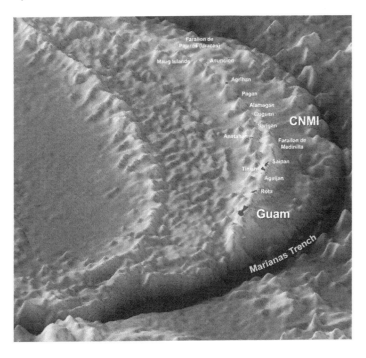

At the time of this writing, NBC Nightly News just finished a week-long stay here on Saipan and the Marianas Trench filming, interviewing, diving and creating a piece that aired on April 20, 2009. As we say in Jamaica, "Big tings a gwan!"

You can keep up-to-date with the Monument at globaloceanlegacy.org.

Note 61: And then there was Obama!

Along with the rest of the world, we here on Saipan watched as history was made in the U.S. presidential election.

Ghanaians, Nigerians and Americans on Saipan all love Obama!

The energy was no less palpable via cable here at Bud's Bar on Saipan!

Note 62: Ode to the Garment Factory

The last garment factory is closing
Bid the SEW-ers forever goodbye
And this chapter will end
and we'll turn a new bend
as the end of an era draws nigh

The last garment factory is closing
goes the bitter along with the sweet
Controversy and fraud?
Opportunity abroad?
Stories change with each person you meet

The last garment factory is closing
Some will say not a moment too soon
But from those who worked hard
daily seams and time cards
come the words of a whole different tune

The last garment factory is closing
ask the girls what they thought of it all
Most will say they were glad
for the chance that they had
and are sad that things slowed to a crawl

The last garment factory is closing
off to cheaper, more profit-filled climes
Shall we toast its demise?
Do we seek a reprise?
Or just strive now to make better times?

The last garment factory is closing
what on earth is our island to do?
Let our leaders contrive
a new plan to survive
so the nation can flourish anew!

The last garment factory is closing
let us hope now the future is kind
Let the Saipan of past
be re-shaped and recast
in an image that let's us all shine!

Just a few short years ago, the Saipan economy was booming as a result of the activity of the garment factories on island. At the same time, Saipan's image and identity have been somewhat tarnished by the media reports, accusations and realities of those very same factories. It's fascinating to hear and contrast what those who are actually working in factories have to say with what is typically reported in the media.

Many of the (predominantly Chinese) women I've interviewed, have expressed a fairly consistent opinion of life as garment factory workers: They appreciate the chance to earn more money here than they could in their home countries; they feel the resident population doesn't like them being here; but they would like to keep working here because of the money, and a certain freedom they have that is hard to find back home, that they've grown accustomed to life here, and that would actually make reintegrating into Chinese society more difficult.

The peaks and valleys of the 25 years of garment factory operations here on Saipan is a story well worth telling--from as many perspectives as possible. The industry's pivotal, and undeniable role and impact on Saipan's current reputation, brand identity, and image is worthy of analysis, as we strive to recreate that reputation and identity in the years ahead.

This has and continues to be a pivotal month of change. Over the span of just a few days we will have witnessed the declaration of the Mariana Trench Marine National Monument (Jan 6), the closure of the last garment factory (Jan 15), a final determination on the Guam-CNMI Visa waiver program (Jan 16), MLK Day (Jan 19) made more poignant and timely given Barack Obama's game-changing inauguration (Jan 20), all within the framework of a continuing economic crisis. Yes, this is the right time. Change is in the air both here and abroad. Are you ready?

The "Ode to the Garment Factory" life rhyme is a reminder that every change comes with different opinions and perspectives, impacts, and (at least) two sides to every issue that, if overlooked, lessen the lesson we can learn by incorporating everyone's viewpoint. "The Last Garment Factory" is Closing is a metaphor for life's periods of transition, for seeking out others' perspectives, and of moving forward armed with a renewed sense of purpose to seek out new options, and make things better than they were before.

There is always opportunity amid change.

I was fortunate enough to arrange a brief look inside "the last garment factory on Saipan," and came away with some historic photos and videos. Here are workers inside Una Moda factory just a few days before it shut its doors forever.

The final factory girls at Uno Moda, Saipan

Uno Moda, Saipan

Note 63: Some Scenes We May not See Again

The garment factories brought with them a host of ladies and men from China, Thailand, Vietnam, the Philippines and other Pacific islands. As the factories close, and workers move back home, or to other regions, there are some familiar sights here on Saipan that will go with them. The cultural events, the celebrations, the languages, and the very energy and soul of certain parts of the island will be affected by their departure. The truth is, this is not unique to life on Saipan. Because of its location, its relationship to the military establishment, the labor laws, and such, Saipan lends itself to frequent comings and goings. The migrant workforce, nomads, tourists, expatriates, military personnel come, stay for a while, then leave. It's something one must get used to if one decides to stay and call Saipan home.

Bicycling with umbrella in the San Antonio sun

Note 64: Chicken Feathers and Garlic Skin

Speaking of factory workers, there was one young lady who has been on Saipan for nine years as a garment factory worker, who I helped to write her memoirs. It's entitled *Chicken Feathers and Garlic Skin: Diary of a Chinese Garment Factory Girl on Saipan* by Chun Yu Wang, as told to Walt Goodridge.

From Saipan factory girl...

... to international author: Chun Yu Wang and the first copy of her book

I'm very honored and proud to have been able to document and publish an experience that many people would never know about. It is the only known chronicle of what it was like to be a garment factory worker on Saipan.

Note 65: Federalization and the Visa Waiver Thing

Breaking News from Saipan!

The latest big news here on Saipan is the anticipated implementation of Federal labor and immigration laws in the CNMI. Here's the overview, in a nutshell.

Even though the CNMI has ostensibly been self-governing, its agreement with the United States has always given the US the right to take over and implement US immigration and labor laws at any time. That time is now. Legislation passed during the Bush administration empowers the Department of Homeland Security to enforce "The Consolidated Natural Resources Act of 2008."

The reason this act is so important to the interests of Saipan and the CNMI is that it includes a change in the requirements that Chinese and Russian tourists need to meet in order to come to Saipan as tourists. At present, and until the full implementation of the act, Chinese and Russians—who make up a small, but growing segment of Saipan's tourists—do not need to apply for a visa to gain entry to Saipan. In other words, their visa requirement is "waived."

However, if and when the act is passed, the new requirements it will mean that Chinese and Russians must apply for and secure tourist visas in order to enter the CNMI.

Many people believe this will have a detrimental effect on the tourism industry.

The second reason this act is so important to the interests of Saipan and the CNMI is that it contains language and laws that further restrict and change the status of contract workers here on island, may separate families which include foreign contract parents of Saipan-born (and therefore) US citizens.

There's a lot more to the story. You can stay informed by visiting the Saipan Tribune website, dhs.gov and destinationsaipan.com

LATEST NEWS: As of April 5, 2009: SAIPAN, Northern Mariana Islands (AP) — US Homeland Security Secretary Janet Napolitano has delayed full implementation of a law mandating the federal takeover of immigration on Saipan, CNMI.

Note 66: The Truth About Saipan!

The following appears on my SaipanLiving.com site.

If you're like me, a title like "The Truth About [Anything]" is a compelling one that makes you want to read more. I believe we all, on some level, yearn to know the truth. Especially if you've heard contrasting things about life on Saipan, it would be nice, once and for all, to get to the truth of it all, wouldn't it?

The truth is, however, there is no single truth about Saipan. In any attempt to uncover the truth, what we find are subjective perspectives, opinions and observations determined by individual agendas. Some agendas are simple: *(eg. "I want to make everyone as miserable as I am").* Some agendas are complex. *(eg. "We will organize a federal takeover, reshape it in our image, and make this a military R&R spot for the troops.")*

Even the news media has an agenda. People joke that the media's motto is "never let the truth get in the way of a good story!" Good (read salacious) stories sell papers, magazines and advertising. Yes, the truth changes based on who is speaking and what they want out of life.

So, whether Saipan is a paradise or a den of corruption is all based on one's agenda. If you are a pessimist who wants people to wallow in your misery, then Saipan is one thing. If you're an optimist, bent on helping improve conditions it's another. If you call yourself a "realist" (generally a pessimist in disguise), then things generally tend toward the negative with the disclaimer that you're just being real.

But that's all okay, because if you know a person's agenda, then everything they say and do makes sense (unless their agenda is specifically to confuse you about what their agenda is; or unless they're just crazy). And, if you know a person's agenda, then you won't be unduly misled by their claims to truth.

Walt's Agenda

So, with that said, what's MY agenda? As the author of several passionpreneur books, and as evidenced by the title of my weekly column, my agenda is to encourage people to start their own businesses based on their passions. However, I have other agendas as well. One is to help ALL peoples optimize their assets, achieve empowerment, and maintain control over the things that matter to them. Here on Saipan—for my own selfish reasons—I'd like to maintain the cultural diversity, natural beauty, and uncomplicated lifestyle that I've come to love about living here.

But wait, there's more. There's also a part of my agenda that some may consider subversive, and that is to reveal the underlying deception of most modern ideals and belief systems, encourage a lifestyle that values simplicity and minimalism instead of consumerism, and excess, that favors the natural over the artificial, and at the same time honors everyone's right and freedom to choose whichever lifestyle works for them.

My goal is to help people arrive at a set of choices that creates a clean environment, promotes optimal health, safeguards the rights and freedoms of all, and offers an effective understanding of reality.

Every column I write, every website I launch, every project I embark upon includes a combination of some or all of those agendas. But don't be misled. Remember my agenda. It's not my nature to focus on the negative, however "real" the realists say it is. People who harp on doom won't start businesses or see the opportunity in the "doom."

Even my "facts" are selectively offered based on my agenda and what I want you to see. I can strive for a 50-50 balance, but even then, I'll always tend to give at least 51% (accentuate the positive, and eliminate the negative, as Bing Crosby sang) to aid the possibility of victory and the triumph of hope.

The Truth About Saipan
So, with that said, here is my truth about Saipan:

• Saipan is overcoming a branding challenge. In other words, what comes to mind when people think of "Saipan" isn't always what those of us who actually live and work here think are its best assets. We're emerging from the shadow of an era tainted by a controversial garment industry, and other bad (accurate or not) press.

• Like the rest of the world, there's an economic transition happening on Saipan. In addition, there are agendas for immigration and labor reform, which make this an island on the verge.

However, even with these and other changes and challenges, there are a multitude of assets which make this a great place to visit, vacation, live, learn and love!

- *Great Weather*—Saipan holds the Guinness World Record for most consistent temperature. The average difference between night and day is greater than the average difference between winter and summer. Those of us who actually live and work here on Saipan enjoy warm tropical weather year round.

- *Natural beauty*--there is natural, pristine beauty here in the form of beautiful sunrises, beaches, foliage, fruits, sunsets, rock formations, aquatic life and more!

- *Proximity to Marianas Trench (the deepest part of the world's oceans)*--while no one actually goes diving that deep, our proximity to such a rich, bio-diverse, unexplored region of the world's oceans has blessed us with underwater life that makes Saipan one of the best places for….

- *World class diving*-- World class shore diving, "Eagle Ray City", and the Grotto are just some of the activities and locations those who dive our waters rave about. We're got a good thing going!

- *Discovery of Ecological significance*—Scientists and students of ecology can learn much about life on our planet from our coral reefs (estimated value comparable to Hawaii), and the pristine, biodiversity of our waters. The US Government recently created the Marianas Trench Marine National Monument (an area of over 12,000 square nautical miles) in recognition of this significance.

- *Cultural diversity*—Life on Saipan has been influenced by the Spanish, Germans, Japanese, and Americans! The indigenous Chamorro and Carolinian people, immigrants, guest workers, tourists, investors and students from Asia, the Pacific, and America, make this a place of unprecedented cultural/ethnic potential.

- *Historical significance*—Without needing to glorify war and violence, it stands as fact that Saipan was key battle site during World War II. It's been said the cold war started in Tinian, the island just 3 miles south of Saipan! That's where the atomic bombs dropped on Japan were launched!

- *Archeological significance*—ancient artifacts of some of the planet's earliest civilizations are found here.

- *Unsolved Mysteries*—The case could be made that there are stories waiting to be told about the Amelia Earhart Mystery, sunken Spanish treasure ships, World War II disappearances, ancient civilizations in which Saipan figures prominently. What might you discover on your own?

And that's just some of the truth about Saipan. (Don't forget my agenda). Despite its challenges, many who come, stay. Many who leave, miss it terribly. And many who travel the world over, come back to enjoy a way of life they can't find anywhere else. Those who actually live and work on Saipan know this to be truth.

"Come See For Yourself!"

Ultimately, the only way to discover the truth about Saipan, is to come see for yourself! But it would be wise to heed the moral of this story:

Once upon a time, a person moved into a new town and asked one of the town residents, "What are the people in this town like?"

"What were the people like in the town you just left?" The resident asked back.

The new person answered, "They were unfriendly and nasty."

And the town resident said, "I think you'll find the people here are just about the same."

Later, the same resident was approached by another new arrival, who asked the same question. Again, the resident asked, "What were the people like in the town you just left?"

The answer was "The people were warm and friendly." And the resident answered, "I think you'll find the people here are just about the same."

Saipan Living Invitation

As founder of SaipanLiving.com, I receive questions and inquiries every day from people who are considering moving to Saipan to live, work, start businesses, rent property, escape the rat race, or simply live a different lifestyle. If you'd like to share your truth with them, as the content on the site is being developed, please visit www.saipanliving.com and/or email me to become an expert and answer their questions. I encourage you to participate, otherwise, their perception of Saipan will be "the world according to Walt," (and who wants a bunch of subversive, minimalist, Jamaican, vegan idealists running around island?)

Note 67: And FINALLY…..A Better Life?

As this edition of *Jamaican On Saipan* was heading to press, I received an order and this email from a woman in the states:

"My boyfriend is moving to Saipan this summer. He has lived in Japan before, but I have always lived stateside. I was in search of books about Americans escaping to a better life. I just knew there had to be something out there…"

"Escaping to a better life," she said. So, I asked myself the obvious questions: *Am I living a better life? and Does Saipan offer a better life?* The answers to those questions are highly subjective and will change with each person you ask. The question comes at a unique time when locals are heading to the mainland US states or Guam for more opportunity. It comes while guest workers are hanging on here hoping for green cards and pathways to US citizenship. It comes while friends of mine who ventured to New York, returned to finally recognize the paradise they left behind.

For some Saipan can be a haven to escape to. For others it can be a hell to escape from. And while I haven't, and don't make a habit of, harping on what others may call the negative aspects of life here, there are, in fact, negatives. (Again, it's all subjective, but yes, there are all the usual vices perpetrated by the usual suspects here too, and they may just *seem* more pronounced since this is a small town, and people don't expect or perhaps, are more emotionally affected by having their "paradise" tainted by some of the same negative aspects of life they left behind.)

Saipan, a better life? That all depends on what you want out of life. By now, you know that *better* for me, has nothing to do with job opportunities, air conditioning, the availability of restaurants and supermarkets offering the standard American diet, not even reliable electrical power! It revolves around my ability to live a simple, uncomplicated life in the company of friendly people.

At the time of this writing, word came from Washington that Department of Homeland Security just delayed the federalization of Saipan's immigration system. But, if and when it eventually happens, what might the federalization of Saipan bring? Will it bring to an end the diversity and multi-ethnic experience that many like about Saipan? Will it mean an end to the paradise, as I and others describe it? Will it end or improve the "better life" that others have found here? Only time will tell. But for now....(raise your cup)....and let's offer a toast....to paradise!

Note 68: The Final, Final Word

....and he disappeared into his dream. And they never saw him again. The End.

I've always wanted to write a book and end it with that line, but as much as I'd like to, I have an obligation to my fellow Jamaican, vegan, entrepreneur nomads out there (all 3 of us) to continue documenting my adventure. So, with that, please enjoy....

The Nomad's Credo

These lines do not define me
for I live beyond the fringe
my sense of who I am
on border guards shall never hinge

My spirit soars unfettered
past the sheltered and the walled
I live a life called freedom
and I go where I am called

I see myself in others
as this world I duly roam
From whence we came we all are one
I call this earth my home

For seeker is my nature
I am wanderer by choice
I plot my life's adventure
as I heed the still small voice...

Next stop: China!

Visit www.JamaicaninChina.com!
and download the free preview (for a limited time)

About the Author

Walt F.J. Goodridge was born in Jamaica and grew up in Old Harbour and Kingston. He attended Old Harbour Primary and Pembroke Hall Primary before his family moved to New York City.

A graduate of Springfield Gardens High School and then Columbia University, Walt is a former civil engineer who walked away from his career to follow his passion for music, writing, and helping others. He has been an artist manager, radio dj, record label owner, inventor, poet, network marketer and consultant.

While attending Columbia University, he was "Sir Walt" hosting the *Reggae Riddims* radio show on WKCR-FM.

He is author of 15 books including *Turn Your Passion Into Profit: A Step-By-Step Guide For Turning ANY Hobby, Talent, Interest Or Idea Into A Money-Making Venture.*

He is also creator of over 468 unique "life rhymes," motivational poems of the thoughts that create success. He has written for *Entrepreneur Magazine* and *Black Enterprise*, and has been featured in *Time Magazine, Wall Street Journal Online, the Dallas Morning News, The Kip Business Report* and numerous publications and websites. Walt offers personalized coaching and conducts workshops around the country to help others make money doing what they love!

Contact Walt at P.O. Box 503991, Saipan, MP 96950, or via email at Walt@saipanliving.com.

Further Reading and Resources

- For the ongoing story of my life in paradise, along with business tips to succeed at your own sideline business, visit *Side Orders: the Money on the Side Business & Lifestyle Blog* www.passionprofit.com/blog

- Learn about BeautifyCNMI! at www.beautifycnmi.com

- Follow Angelo Villagomez' adventures: Thesaipanblogger.com

- Meet the diverse and interesting members of the amazing WeLoveSaipan Network, check out www.welovesaipan.com

- See all my Saipan-centered websites at www.BestofSaipan.com

Ready to discover Saipan for yourself? Let me give you a special "Walt's Tour of Saipan" as described on DiscoverSaipan.com, and, book your accommodations at DestinationSaipan.com!

Saipan on DVD!

Check out these DVDs for more about Saipan, it's people, culture and beauty, created by Saipanpreneurs here on island!

Lieweila: A Micronesian Story: Narrated by Cinta Kaipat, a descendant of the first migrants, the film tells the history of the Refalawasch people beginning with details of the early migrations and ending with their current situation on Saipan. *($27.00)*

State of Liberty: Looking for America, is the pilot episode of a series which captures life, love and the pursuit of happiness here on Saipan. Filmmaker Dan Shor states: *"it's a story about the microcosm of the world that populates this tiny little island. Our lead characters are Japanese, Chinese, Chamorro, Carolinian, Bangladeshi, Filipino, Russian, and stateside Americans."*

Everyone is represented, even the Jamaican(s) on the island. (No I wasn't in it, but much of the music in the soundtrack is none other than that unmistakable drum and bass of Reggae!) *($20.00)*

The Underwater World of Saipan is a 105-minute DVD showcasing the incredible beauty and bio-diversity of Saipan's underwater world. This DVD takes you on 7 distinctly different dives including The Grotto, Obyan, Banzai Cliff, Ice Cream, Managaha, Naftan Point and Lau Lau Bay. *($25.00)*

Order these and other unique gifts at
www.saipanpreneur.com

Saipan in paperback

Chicken Feathers and Garlic Skin: *Diary of a Chinese Garment Factory Girl on Saipan* by Chun Yu Wang, as told to Walt Goodridge

It took a lot of courage for a 25-year-old girl from Wu Xi City in Jiang Shu province, China, who had never flown on a plane, and who had never left home before, to travel 2,000 miles to a foreign country in search of work. It took even more courage to stay once she discovered what life was really like for a factory girl on the island of Saipan in the US Commonwealth of the Northern Mariana Islands (CNMI).

Did she make the greatest mistake of her life? Like many girls, she came with dreams of a better future. Yes, the pay was better than in China, but at what price? Would the high pressure of 15-hour quota-driven days of tedious, mind and finger-numbing work get to her? Or would the greedy floor monitors, and scam-artists preying on lonely, naive women rob her not just of her income, but of her innocence as well? At every turn, there were *wolves ahead and tigers behind* that threatened her dreams of happiness. Could she learn Saipan's secret factory system and get ahead before she lost it all? Could she save money, save face, and return to China better off? Would she even want to, given the *real* reason she left China in the first place? (www.saipanfactorygirl.com)

Books and Products by Walt F.J. Goodridge
(most are available in ebook, and paperback formats)

Turn Your Passion Into Profit (ebook, paperback, 6-CD)
The Tao of Wow
The Ageless Adept
Change the Game
Hip Hop Entrepreneur Lists of Exposure
This Game of Hip Hop Artist Management
Life Rhymes for the Passion-Centered Life
Come into Our Whirl
Lessons in Success
Hip Hop Profits
The Hip Hop Record Label Business Plan
The Niche Market Report
Chicken Feathers and Garlic Skin
Jamaican on Saipan
Doing Business on Saipan
Living True to Your Self

a complete product list, along with articles, free reports and a passion personality test are available at www.passionprofit.com

Quiz! Yes, a Quiz!
Oops! Didn't I tell you there'd be a quiz afterwards?

Interspersed throughout the pages of *Jamaican On Saipan*, and woven seamlessly into the commentary and dialogue are the titles and lyrics of some of the most popular and classic Reggae songs of all time. How many of you true Jamaicans found the names of at least 10 popular Jamaican songs in the text of this book?

For example, on page 14, in the second paragraph:

"I bought my ticket, gave away my 2500-strong vinyl lp collection, donated my books to a combination of friends and street vendors, unloaded almost <u>everything I own</u>, and jetted."

"Everything I Own" is the title of Reggae singer Ken Boothe's classic cover of Bread's "Everything I Own" from 1972.

Think you found all ten? Or more? Send an email to answers@jamaicanonsaipan for an autoresponse with the answers!

Order for yourself or for someone you love

"Once upon a time, there was this Jamaican guy who hated his job, followed his passion, started a sideline business self-publishing his own "how to" e-books, made enough money to quit his civil engineering career, ran away to a tropical island in the South Pacific, and started a tourism business so he could give tours of the island to pretty girls every day! Walt Goodridge is Jamaican on Saipan!

Please send ____ copies of *Jamaican On Saipan!* to:
1 copy = $14.95 + $5.00 shipping and handling = $19.95
2 copies = 29.90 + 5.50 shipping/handling = $34.90
3 copies = $44.85 + $6.00 shipping/handling = $50.85

Name _____ Telephone _____

Address _____

City _____ State ____ Zip/Postal code ____

Email Address _____

Please make checks or money orders payable to and mail to:

                The Passion Profit Company

                     c/o Walt Goodridge

                      PO Box 503991

                     Saipan MP 96950

      If ordering as a gift, please include your name below

Giver's (Your) Name _____

Or, you may order copies for friends and family at
www.JamaicanOnSaipan.com

Made in the USA
Middletown, DE
18 December 2014